CSI

in the Classroom

Everything You Need to Plan and Teach a Successful CSI Unit in Any Subject

by Jessica Pless

Incentive Publications
Nashville, Tennessee

Illustrated by Kathleen Bullock
Cover by Robert Voigts
Edited by Marjorie Frank
Copy-edited by Cary Grayson

ISBN 978-0-86530-672-1

1   2   3   4   5   6   7   8   9   10   12   11   10   09

PRINTED IN THE UNITED STATES OF AMERICA
www.incentivepublications.com

Contents

SCENE DO NOT CROSS LINE CRIME SCENE DO NO

What is CSI in the Classroom?

CSI in the Classroom is an experience that uses investigation skills, forensic analysis, and many other skills and processes—approximating the work of real-life investigators and scientists. The teacher designs a crime and sets up a crime scene, enlisting the help of other adults in the school. Students first gain some forensics experience; then they investigate and solve the crime. In doing this, they use an impressive range of cross-curricular skills to follow the evidence, explain what happened, and identify the culprit.

How did CSI in the Classroom come about?

It's hard to miss the phenomenon! Across the world, people of all ages are fascinated with the idea that even the most minute, ordinary, or unexpected evidence can lead to solving a crime. CSI in the Classroom takes its clues from the popularity of the CSI television programs and other programs based on forensic science.

*As a middle-school teacher, I noticed this excitement about forensic investigations and the way the idea has exploded across the media in both fictional and nonfictional genres. So, with the assistance of a deputy police chief, I created CSI experiences in my own classroom.
I did this to bring rich, realistic, cross-curricular experiences to my students.*

I believed that the CSI concept would motivate students. I guessed that they would be more committed to their schoolwork if they could connect it to something real, relevant, and captivating. I was right! Students who have been a part of classroom CSI units have shown high involvement and remarkable achievement in the related learning processes and skills.

After seeing the results with my own students, I shared the CSI model with friends and colleagues, who have used it with success. So I went on to write this book to show other teachers how to make the CSI experience come alive (and work) for their students.

Jessica L. Pless

During a CSI unit, students work cooperatively in teams to:

- plan an investigation;

- collect, examine, and discuss evidence;

- put forensic skills to work analyzing clues from the crime scene;

- comb through, photograph, and diagram the crime scene;

- follow legal procedures to obtain and examine evidence;

- track down suspects, create questions, interview suspects and victims, and take statements;

- keep notes and write reports;

- make inferences and draw conclusions about what evidence means; and

- use evidence and sound reasoning to solve the crime.

Call for Crime Scene Investigation!

It's Monday morning. Students in the first-period P.E. class at Scranton Middle School have just arrived at the gym. They are transfixed by the sight. Strewn across the floor are dozens of deflated balls: basketballs, soccer balls, volleyballs, footballs, kickballs—even tennis balls. In fact, the teacher soon discovers that the air has been let out of every single ball from the equipment room. He stops the class at the edge of the gym. As they stare, some notice muddy footprints, empty soda cans, a scrap of a homework paper, and gum wrappers amidst the mess.

On that same morning in the next county, another strange crime situation is uncovered. Mr. Gear, first to arrive at Gardner Middle School that morning, is faced with a mess in the front foyer. The trophy case is turned on its side, the door is ajar, and the prized Soccer Championship trophy (the largest trophy of them all) is missing. Mr. Gear immediately notices the broken mirror, dried red drops (that appear to be blood), clumps of mud, an open (chewed-on) taffy bar, and hundreds of green jellybeans that litter the floor.

Down the hall, a group of sixth graders spill into their geography classroom as the bell rings. The teacher starts the class by pulling down the world map. But the map looks strange. It has been rearranged and changed. The scale, key, and title of the map are all different. All the continents are in the wrong places! On close inspection, Mrs. Thomas sees that someone has cut shapes of continents and other features and taped them over the original map. A roll of tape, scissors, paper scraps, Tootsie Rolls, and a note reading, "Dentist appt after school" are discovered at the front corner of the classroom.

Call for CSI !

On the other side of the city, at Highlander Way Middle School, Mrs. Carr's second-period science class has just finished cleaning up from an experiment. In rushes the football coach. Waving his arms and speaking at an unusually fast pace, he reports that the school mascot's uniform is hanging from the goal post out on the football field. He tells about some other unusual things on the field: chunks of torn fabric caught on one pole, a CD apparently dropped at the scene, a note taped to the goal post, and a half-eaten hotdog on the ground nearby.

In a nearby state, Mr. Atherton returns from lunch duty to set up for his sixth-period pre-algebra class at Pattengill Middle School. To his surprise, he finds that all the calculators, which were kept in a box in his locked cupboard, have been set out on the desks. The cupboard door is open. The lock is lying on the floor. Curiously, every calculator is upside down, and every battery has been removed. The batteries are nowhere to be seen, but a strange white powder, candy wrappers, and the strong odor of perfume are evident.

An unused locker is the scene of a mystery across the state at Hartland Junior High. A custodian hears music coming from the girls' locker room when he returns to work after the holiday break. He heads that way to check it out, surprised because it is too early for anyone to have arrived at school. As he approaches, he recognizes the song, "Who Let the Dogs Out?" But the music is not what startles him the most when he enters the room. It is the strong, rotten smell and the oozing liquid flowing in front of one of the lockers. He pries off the lock, and out falls a huge mesh bag of rotting tomatoes. Sticky footprints, scraps of pizza crust, and a soggy notebook might turn out to be useful clues.

Across the country at Clark Academy, everyone has been excited about the upcoming fundraiser. Students have been taking orders for two weeks for the caramel corns and popcorns of various flavors. The school's order of popcorn arrived last week—all 900 bags! The money has been collected, and today is the day the packages are to be delivered by students to the buyers. Imagine the student-council president's horror when he goes into the storage room to get the boxes and finds them all open with most of the popcorn gone! Chocolate caramel corn crumbs litter the floor. A scissors, a ball cap, and mysterious paper strips seem to have been left behind by the culprit or culprits.

Crime Scene Investigation is spreading to classrooms across the country!

Join in on the fun and the learning opportunities!

Call for CSI!

Why Use CSI in Your Classroom?

Here are a few of the many good reasons to set up a CSI unit in your classroom.

CSI takes skills!

reading for information
comprehending
writing
following directions
outlining
interviewing
organizing and planning
summarizing
paraphrasing
measuring, calculating
applying prior knowledge
questioning
observing
examining and reexamining
hypothesizing
inferring
predicting
checking predictions
drawing conclusions
analyzing
synthesizing
making judgments
evaluating
arguing
recording
communicating
interviewing
reporting
creating
cooperating
collaborating, discussing
taking care of supplies
managing self-behavior

1. CSI motivates students to learn!

A host of respectable research studies tell us that, when students are motivated, these improve: academic achievement, attitudes about learning, attendance, and classroom behavior. Furthermore, research confirms that motivation is increased when learning experiences involve:

cooperation and collaboration with others
challenging tasks
problem solving and decision making
independence and self-reliance
relevance to the student's life
use of prior knowledge
pursuit of a fascinating idea
opportunities to build confidence
choices
fun

A classroom CSI includes ALL of these factors!

2. CSI uses a wide range of skills.

A classroom unit in CSI involves learning at many levels. See the list (at left) of some of the skills and processes that are strengthened when students plunge into crime-scene investigations. These are the kinds of learning outcomes you can expect from your CSI unit.

3. CSI is for all subject areas.

CSI skills cross all curricular areas. Even better, CSI integrates knowledge and critical thinking skills needed for many disciplines. Don't shy away from a CSI unit because you are not a science teacher. This can work for and enhance any subject area.

4. Students love CSI.

They'll remember the experience long after it's over. They'll beg for more CSI! Who knows, some students might even be inspired to become detectives, forensic scientists, judges, prosecutors, or investigative reporters!

How to Use This Book

This book gives step-by-step procedures for planning and implementing a crime-scene investigation in your classroom or building. The user-friendly structure is easy to follow, with plenty of templates, forms, checklists, and agendas. This is the help you need for creating your own CSI classroom experience! It's all here: planning and preparation tools, forensic prelabs to prepare students for analysis of evidence, bulletin board ideas, passes for leaving the class, ID badges for students, assessment forms, and sample scenarios that are easily adapted to your situation.

There are many ways to use the book. Choose those that fit your students, their needs, your schedule, and your style.

• Turn one forensic prelab into a mini-CSI unit.

Find some "evidence" for students to observe, test, and analyze. Challenge them to draw conclusions from the results.

• Use all the forensic prelabs throughout the year.

Without planning a full-scale CSI unit, simply use the prelabs as a way to introduce students to some of the science and skills of crime-scene investigation. You can even turn each lab into a mini-CSI.

• Turn one of the CSI activities into a mini-lesson.

Set up a simple crime scene; then let students collect the evidence and log it. Or have students photograph and sketch a crime scene and draw inferences from looking at these. Or, find someone who will pose as a witness to an event, and make a lesson of writing interview questions and conducting interviews with the witness.

• Plan a simple crime-scene investigation.

Use tools and resources from the book to plan a simple CSI unit, using minimal clues, suspects, and steps to a solution.

• Follow the book as a guide for a longer CSI unit.

Use the book as a step-by-step guide, following one of the suggested scenarios or developing your own.

• Adapt the ideas to your own CSI plan.

Take the ideas that fit your students and your situation. Add, subtract, rearrange, and expand until you get the CSI plan that will work for your classroom.

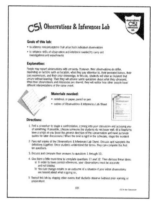

Teacher information pages are identified by the black triangle in the outside upper corner.

Crime-scene tape identifies pages for students and CSI teams.

Student pages in the CSI prelabs can be identified by the spiral binding.

9

To make the best use of this book:

1. Get familiar with the CSI idea.

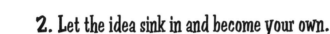

Start by reviewing the entire book to get the scope and idea of a classroom CSI. As you read, you will see processes, recommendations, and tools provided by a teacher who started from scratch and came up with a good plan for making this work. Take time to look at each section until you understand how it works.

2. Let the idea sink in and become your own.

Mull over the concept and start thinking about how it could take shape in your classroom or school. Think about crime scenarios that might work, places for crime scenes, and details that would fit your setting and your students. Think about skills from your subject area that could be worked into a CSI scenario.

3. Consider how to fit a classroom CSI into your schedule.

As you read through the CSI steps, think about how and when you can fit this into your schedule. Don't pass up a chance for doing CSI because you feel it is an "extra" thing to do on top of your other teaching responsibilities. It is not extra! It includes the very things you need to teach anyway. Think of it as a way for students to master some of those same skills and standards with more involvement, greater relevance, and enhanced motivation.

4. Get others involved.

Share the idea with team members, colleagues, school staff members, and parents. Get together and talk about how you can make this work in your school. Build a support base before you start a classroom CSI.

5. Start simple; then build.

Start with one class, a few of the CSI activities, or a simple scenario. You can always develop a more complex unit on your next try.

6. Be flexible.

This book is a guide, not a concrete plan. Adapt the details to create your own specific plan. Remember to do what works for your students, you, and your schedule.

> The idea is **NOT** just to create a mystery that students think about, read about, and talk about.
> The idea is to use **REAL** forensic investigation to solve a crime.

Planning Your CSI

CRIME SCENE DO NOT CROSS CRIME SCENE DO NOT CR

How to Plan a CSI Unit

Our Own CSI (Planning Templates)

Sample CSI Scenarios

1 The Case of the
Stolen Treasure Box

2 The Case of the
Pilfered Pig

3 The Case of the
Missing Spelling Bee Plaque

plan a
CSI
unit

How to Plan a CSI Unit

A few weeks before the CSI begins:

1. Choose a crime scenario.

Look around your school for something meaningful to students—something that would cause alarm if it disappeared. For example:

- the school mascot (or uniform)
- a CD with plans for the eighth-grade field trip
- the pizza ingredients in the kitchen
- important sheet music for an upcoming concert
- a special school trophy, banner, or award
- the school yearbook CD ready for print
- all the maps from the geography classrooms
- the basketball team's new uniforms
- an expensive new video camera from the drama club
- the candy bars recently purchased for a fundraising event

OR, think of something that would cause alarm if it were vandalized or if it unexpectedly showed up on school grounds. For example:

- a broken trophy case with missing trophies
- damaged P.E. equipment (all the air let out of the balls)
- a rotting roast beef in a locker
- confetti all over the cafeteria
- a goat tied to a goal cage on the soccer field
- a lawnmower left in the principal's office

Are you still stumped for an idea?

Think about treasured belongings of the organizations in your building: student government, yearbook or newspaper, music groups and bands, clubs, and sports teams. Or think about places, spaces, or belongings important to a cook, volunteer, custodian, coach, teacher, counselor, secretary, or principal.

If you need more help, see sample CSI cases on pages 6–7 and 21–32. Get ideas from them, or adapt one to make it work for you.

Have fun!

2. Create the details of the scenario.

- Once you have decided on the crime, write an outline or list of all the details. Plan the roles of the victims (people who first report the crime or major crime evidence), the guilty suspect(s), and the other suspects. Use the planning templates on pages 16–18.

- If this is your first CSI in the classroom, keep your scenario simple. Start with just one class. Limit the number of clues to be analyzed, and perhaps limit the number of suspects also.

- Think about clues that will be left at the crime scene(s) for students to find and analyze. Plan ways that these clues can be tied to specific suspects. Deliberately plan some clues that could connect to more than one suspect. Note the kinds of evidence that students can test using the prelabs explained on pages 101–122.

- Identify an adult victim closely associated with the missing or damaged items or with the crime situation of your invented scenario. (For example, if the crime involves missing or damaged P.E. equipment, the victim might be a coach or the P.E. teacher.) Find a second complainant (victim) who discovers additional evidence later. Choose people who are willing to be informally fingerprinted.

- Find another four to six people in the school who will agree to participate in your scenario as suspects. Use volunteers who could logically be connected to the crime. Try to use at least three of the six who are highly suspicious, with strong reasons to be involved in the crime. Choose people who are willing to be informally fingerprinted.

- Use the CSI Participant Information templates on pages 19–20 to provide details for each suspect or victim. Give them information that includes:

  – where they were at the time of the crime,
  – what they were doing,
  – who might have seen them coming or going,
  – who might have overheard them saying something to someone,
  – and their own thoughts or suspicions about the crime.

Also identify favorite types of ink pens, gum, beverages, perfumes, or other personal preferences that could tie that person to the crime scene. Think of any forensic details that connect suspects to the crime scene(s).

13

3. Plan the crime scene(s).

- Make a careful plan for what each crime scene will contain. (Many CSI scenarios work best with Crime Scene A, where something happened or was stolen, and Crime Scene B, where the missing item was discovered or where some further evidence was discovered.)

- Sketch a diagram or floor plan of each crime scene. This will help you envision the evidence that students will collect. The diagram will also help expedite your set-up of the crime scene(s).

- List materials needed for clues—things such as: hair samples; items of food or objects with teeth marks; notes that show handwriting or typing; gum, pens, footprints, fabrics, fibers, or powders; or any other items or substances that a suspect might leave at a crime scene.

4. Decide on the prelabs you will need.

- After planning the crime, suspects, and clues, review all the prelabs on pages 101–122. Identify the labs you will need to offer to students before the CSI begins. (You may want to do all the prelabs, even though students will not use all the skills in their CSI.)

- Identify supplies needed for prelabs. See a master list on page 98.

5. Plan the CSI kits and the forensic lab.

- Make a clear list of everything students will need for gathering and examining evidence. See the CSI kit described on page 40.

- Review the information about setting up a classroom forensic lab on page 49. Make a list of supplies that will be needed to set up the lab so that it is ready for students to analyze evidence during the CSI.

6. Think about spaces and places.

- Consider the space in your classroom. Decide where you can put a CSI bulletin board, set up the forensic lab, store CSI supplies, and keep team folders. Make sure there is appropriate space for teams to work together.

- Think about all the other places in the school, in addition to the crime scenes, that might be needed for parts of the CSI.

7. Think through every step of your CSI.

- Review the CSI at a Glance (pages 34–36), the CSI Readiness Checklist (page 50), and the CSI Daily Agenda (pages 52–62). These will help you anticipate the key details in your CSI plan. Follow that agenda, or use the planning template (page 63) to make a daily agenda for your own CSI.

- Make a timeline to follow as you prepare for and carry out the CSI in your classroom. Include jobs and deadlines for yourself, the CSI teams, and all the other people involved in the unit.

8. Enlist helpers.

- List all the jobs that can be done by volunteers, including parents. This can include such things as helping to gather supplies ahead of time; coming into the classroom to assist with CSI preparations and activities; or supervising students as they videotape, work in the forensics lab, or perform other tasks that need assistance.

- Give all volunteers clear instructions and schedules regarding their duties.

9. Inform others.

- Think about all the staff members in the school who should be informed about the CSI. Let these people (such as the principal, custodians, security personnel, and secretaries) know what to expect during the CSI.

- Involve students in as many of the preparation tasks as possible. Put them to work making badges, preparing CSI team folders or evidence tags, or setting up the forensics lab. These activities draw students into the excitement and give them a chance to exercise their planning, creative, and artistic skills.

- Make sure that parents understand how they can be involved, why you are doing this, how the CSI will work, and what is expected of the students.

A few other suggestions:

- *Start by taking this book apart! Punch holes in the pages and put it all in a notebook for handy, multiple uses.*

- *Get yourself and your students immersed in the CSI spirit by sharing stories, books, CDs, or resources that follow mystery or detective or investigative themes.*

- *Be prepared to improvise and problem solve as you go along. Things will arise that you did not anticipate.*

- *Don't let all the planning dampen your enthusiasm. You are about to embark on a great adventure!*

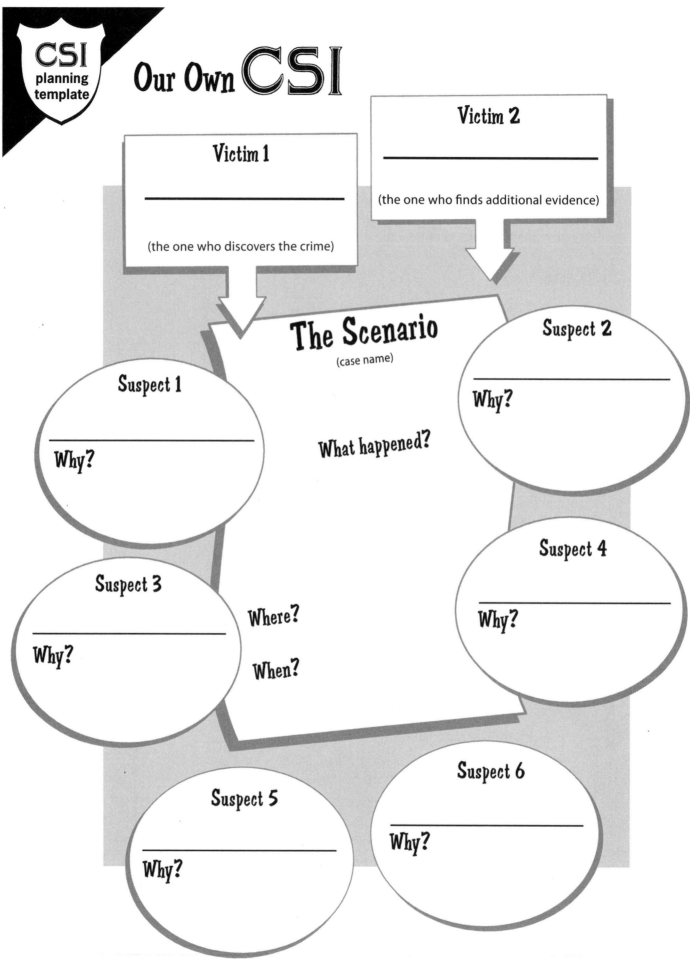

CSI planning template

Our Own CSI

Victim 1

_____

(the one who discovers the crime)

Victim 2

_____

(the one who finds additional evidence)

The Scenario
(case name)

What happened?

Where?

When?

Suspect 1

_____

Why?

Suspect 2

_____

Why?

Suspect 3

_____

Why?

Suspect 4

_____

Why?

Suspect 5

_____

Why?

Suspect 6

_____

Why?

The Crime Scenes

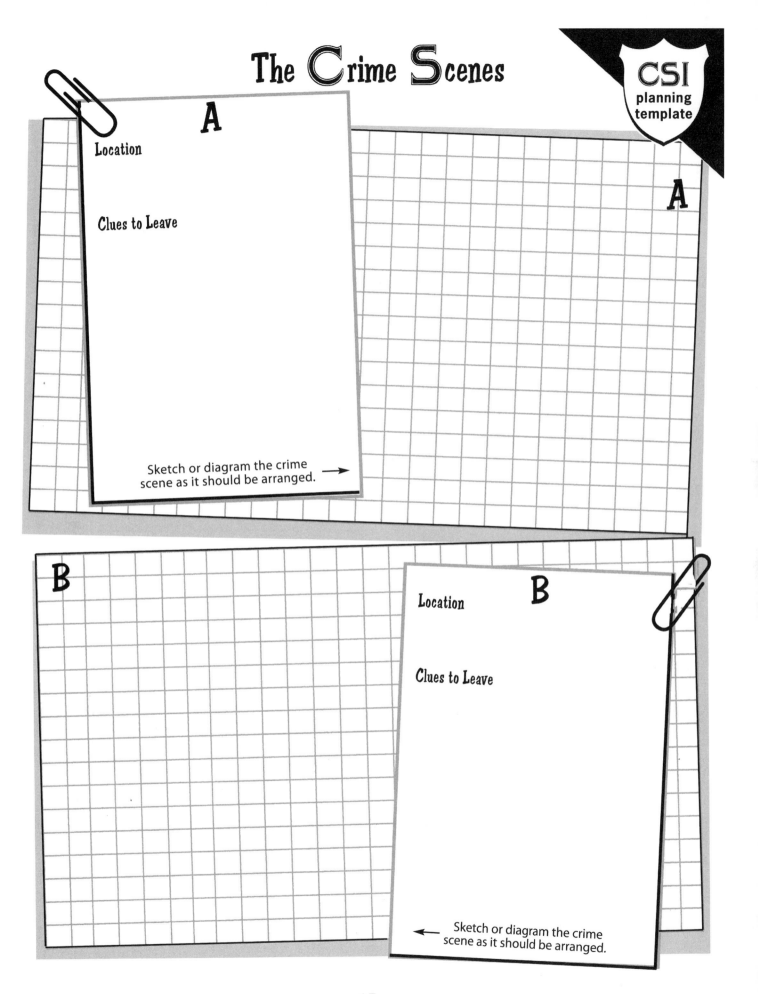

A

Location

Clues to Leave

Sketch or diagram the crime scene as it should be arranged. →

A

B

B

Location

Clues to Leave

← Sketch or diagram the crime scene as it should be arranged.

CSI in the Classroom

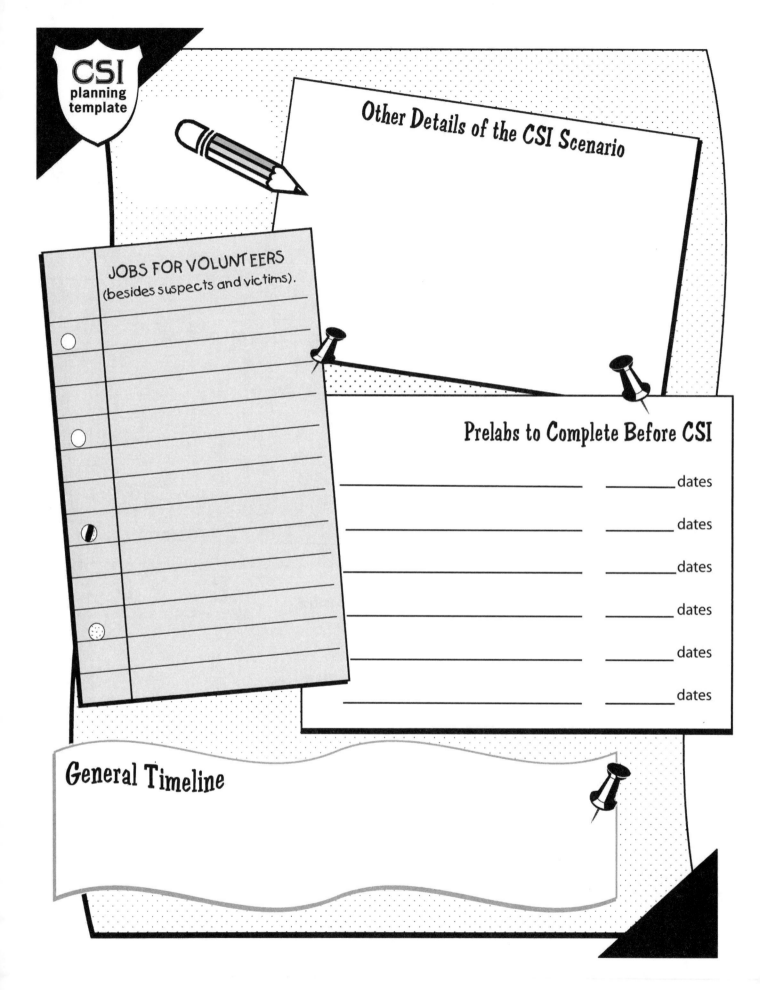

CSI planning template

Other Details of the CSI Scenario

JOBS FOR VOLUNTEERS
(besides suspects and victims).

Prelabs to Complete Before CSI

_____ _____ dates

_____ _____ dates

_____ _____dates

_____ _____ dates

_____ _____ dates

_____ _____ dates

General Timeline

CSI Participant Information

For all CSI Victims and Suspects

Congratulations! You are about to embark on a great adventure as a participant in this crime scene investigation.

Name of the CSI Case:_____

Please remember:

The CSI will begin on _____ and run approximately through_____.
A description of your role is attached. Please review it thoroughly.

When you see a student with a badge in hand,
it is time to get into character and play your role.

Don't let students see these sheets!

CONFIDENTIAL

If a CSI team investigator asks you for fingerprints, a bite impression, a pen, or any other item, make sure he or she gives you an approved search warrant before you honor the request.

Please keep this information confidential. Avoid discussing your role with other staff members.

Please don't give away any information that you learn other than what is given for you personally.

Please give NO hints to students. This is a competition!

Feel free to ask me questions at any time.

Please join our class for final reports and our CSI celebration.
The precise dates and time depend upon the length of the investigation.
We will let you know.

Thank you for your participation and support!

Teacher signature _____

CSI in the Classroom

CSI Role Description

To_____ (name)

Your role will be   ☐ victim (complainant)   ☐ suspect (guilty)

                     ☐ suspect (not guilty)   ☐ other

Your CSI role:

_____ Teacher

The Case of the Stolen Treasure Box

Background:

The Case of the Stolen Treasure Box was a fun scenario centered on the school-wide Literacy Challenge. This was a weekly contest in which students read a chapter or a magazine article and wrote a short "reading review" to share with an adult in the building. Each week the names of several students who had completed these reviews were drawn and shared during morning announcements. Those students got to choose a prize from the all-school treasure box.

The shop teacher had built the teasure box, spending many hours crafting it with beautiful, intricate detail. Most of the prizes were displayed on shelves in a corner of the library, because they were too large for the treasure box.

On a Tuesday morning, the librarian noticed that the treasure box was gone. She immediately went to the main office to announce that the Literacy Challenge would be cancelled until further notice. Then she reported the crime to the classroom with CSI teams in place.

The sixth-grade counselor, known for her kindness and generosity, was in the habit of giving prizes or sweet treats to students to help brighten their day or thank them for doing something nice. Although she was not guilty, she quickly became a suspect when word got out that she gave a few students prizes similar to some of the prizes in the treasure box.

The sixth-grade band teacher also became a suspect when he gave away prizes that same week. (It was merely coincidental, and he had a good explanation for this.)

There was also reason to suspect the shop teacher. After putting so much work into building the treasure box, he was disappointed to see how few of the prizes actually were in the box. Furthermore, it annoyed him that many prizes blocked the view of his lovely box. So he took it to use in his own classroom, thinking it wouldn't be missed. When he saw the uproar caused by the box's disappearance and learned that the box was appreciated after all, he was sorry he had taken it. He left it in an empty office where it was sure to be found. He never expected the CSI investigators to dust for fingerprints!

CSI in the Classroom

sample **CSI** scenario 1

The Case of the Stolen Treasure Box

Roles for Victim and Suspects

Notes:

- *I gave a reminder about the bell schedule to each participant in this case.*

- *Each participant received a copy of the CSI Participant Information sheet and individual role description. See pages 19 and 20 for these templates.*

- *The following pages contain role descriptions given to the participants.*

Note to All CSI Participants
In this CSI, time is important. Please review:

Bell Schedule

First Bell (Welcome Bell) is at 8:10 AM

Second Bell (Warning Bell) is at 8:14 AM

Third Bell (Tardy Bell) School begins at 8:18 AM

Morning Announcements begin at 8:23 AM

Suspect A

(Social Studies Teacher)

You arrive each day at 8:05 AM. You were in the library on Monday for the staff meeting. You support the Literacy Challenge and have donated prizes to it. You think it's a great way to encourage reading. You were not in the library on Tuesday, and you had a substitute on Wednesday.

Suspect B

(Counselor)

You arrive at school each day around 7:45 AM. You have access to the library, you love reading, and you think the Literacy Challenge is a great opportunity to reward students for reading. You yourself reward students often when you catch them doing something thoughtful or working especially hard. You have many small prizes and treasures in your office similar to those in the treasure box. You have even donated prizes to the Literacy Challenge.

On the day the treasure box was stolen, you were in the library at approximately 8:10 AM to return a book. Nobody was in the library when you entered. You put the book in the book drop and left the library to return to your office hallway for morning greetings and hall monitoring. On your way out of the library, you ran into the math teacher who wanted a video. You informed him that the librarian wasn't in for checkout of materials, and proceeded downstairs.

Victim and Suspect C

(Librarian)

You arrive each day at 7:00 AM. You love reading and believe in the Literacy Challenge! You know the treasure box was on the prize shelf on Monday, because you put two new prizes next to it that day. Tuesday morning, you had just arrived at school at 7:00 AM and started checking in books when the band teacher interrupted you, yelling about his missing music. You informed him that you found it after the staff meeting yesterday and put it in his mailbox. He turned around and left the library in a mad dash. You finished checking in books around 7:15 AM and decided to start the coffee pot in the teachers' lounge. A few teachers came in and you chatted awhile about yesterday's staff meeting. You returned to the library for a few minutes, then ran downstairs before your first class to check your mailbox and deliver a book to a sixth-grade teacher. You went back again to the library around 8:15 AM after the first bell rang.

Just before morning announcements, you noticed that the treasure box was gone. Immediately, you went to the office to announce that the Literacy Challenge would be cancelled until further notice because the treasure box was missing. You then contacted the CSI teams to report a possible crime.

When you arrived in the library on Wednesday, you found a note that had been left some time when you were not there. It was a reminder about getting a substitute for Wednesday. You suspect the counselor, the math teacher, or the band teacher of taking the box. This is because they have been rewarding students with prizes since the treasure box disappeared and because they had access to the library Tuesday morning. You do not suspect the shop teacher, as he is the one who made the treasure box.

Suspect D

(Band Teacher)

You arrive at school each morning at 7:00 AM. You tutor band students for an hour before school begins, either for individual help or small-group ensemble practice. On Tuesday, you ran upstairs to the library at 7:01 AM while a student was preparing his instrument and warming up. You were in the library at 7:05 AM looking for your sheet music, which you had left there the day before during a staff meeting. While you looked around for the music, you noticed the librarian checking in books in her back office. You called out to her and asked if she had seen your sheet music. She said she had found it after the staff meeting and put it downstairs in your mailbox. You thanked her and left the library in a mad dash. You were back in your classroom (band room) by 7:15 AM.

You think the Literacy Challenge is important, but music is your passion and you believe that every person should be able to play an instrument of some type. (You repeat this belief every time a student investigator questions you.)

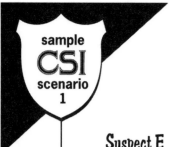

Suspect E

(Math Teacher)

You arrive at school each morning between 8:05 AM and 8:11 AM. You have access to the library all the time. Tuesday morning, you ran up to the library before your first class to get a video for a substitute that would be teaching your classes on Wednesday. Upon entering the library, you passed the counselor who informed you that the librarian was not in, so you turned around to go back to your classroom. But after suddenly realizing that this was the only time you had for getting that video, you turned back to the library, grabbed the case labeled, "Fantastic Fractions," and ran back to class as the first bell rang. Later you realized that while in the library you had dropped a sticky reminder note that was on the clipboard you had been carrying.

You have noticed that students have been working hard in your classes since the Literacy Challenge began. So you have adopted a prize-giving tactic. You have asked local businesses to donate prizes and you have started buying prize items to reward students for their hard work.

Suspect F

(Wood Shop Teacher)

You arrive at school each day around 7:30 AM. You have access to the library any time. You think the Literacy Challenge is a great way to get students to read. You think rewarding students with prizes is great and the treasure box is awesome, but you don't like the fact that it is used for very few prizes. In addition, you are disappointed that the larger prizes sitting on the shelf obscure the box.

You had coffee with the librarian on Tuesday morning around 7:35 AM in the teachers' lounge. At 7:45 AM, you noticed that the librarian was chatting and enjoying coffee with another teacher. You realized that this was your chance to slip into the library to reclaim the treasure box you had crafted. You were sure no one would miss it. You were absent on Wednesday to attend a conference.

The Case of the Pilfered Pig

Background:

My class loved *The Case of the Pilfered Pig!* The victim was a favorite school secretary who had a pig collection in her office. Because anyone who entered could see the pigs easily, this office presented a perfect setting for a CSI scenario.

The pilfered pig was a ceramic white pig with the Canadian flag painted on each side. It was chosen for two reasons: it was easy to lift fingerprints from the ceramic, and it had the Canadian flag on it. This led students to suspect all sixth-grade teachers, since all of them teach about Canada. In addition, suspicion was cast on anyone who had chaperoned the field trip to Niagara Falls, Canada.

A Post-it note left on the floor of an empty office was staged as part of the scenario. This note read, "Call Shirley at 6:00 PM." The note provided an opportunity for students to use chromatography and handwriting labs. Both of these labs would require students to write search warrant affidavits in order to obtain pens or handwriting samples from suspects. The connection to a "Shirley" provided an interview question for investigators.

The suspects who participated in this CSI were all easily accessible throughout each day: secretaries, counselors, our school social worker, and the guilty suspect—one of our school security guards who brought her police dog to school each day.

Crime Scene A, the site of the pig collection, was the Discipline Office on the east side of the building—a place always open and easily accessible by students.

Crime Scene B, where the pig was eventually found, was a small office within the Attendance Office on the west side of our building. Because it was empty, this office was a perfect location to rope off with crime-scene tape. It was left untouched for almost two weeks. The office staff that worked nearby monitored the investigators.

The Case of the Pilfered Pig

Roles for Victim and Suspects

Notes:

- *Each participant received a copy of the CSI Participant Information sheet and individual role description. See pages 19 and 20 for these templates.*

- *The following pages contain role descriptions given to the participants.*

Victim and Suspect A

(Secretary with the Pig Collection)

You love your pig collection! You suspect everyone, as everyone comments about your pigs. You think they are all just jealous because you can display them in your office, can give information about every pig, and can name the occasion and reason for which each pig was given to you.

You know that the white Canada pig was on your desk when you came in the office this morning, because you greet each pig every day when you arrive. Just before second period, you went back to your office after running errands to the main office and the mailroom. This is when you noticed that your favorite pig was missing.

When investigators ask about your pig collection, choose any pig, give elaborate details about the pig, and tell a story about it. If students ask you again, tell them a different story about the same pig (who gave it to you, when, and why). This will confuse them!

If asked, report that you don't like dogs. Tell investigators that the school security guard often brings her dog into the school to do security checks, and regularly stops in the office. At these times, you sharply command her to get the dog out of your office! Make other comments that could lead investigators to take note of your dislike for dogs.

If asked, tell them that you always use a black pen for documents and reports that you complete.

Your daughter's name is Shirley.

Suspect B

(Sixth-grade Teacher)

You have access to the east office. You don't like the secretary's pig collection because it clutters her desk and offers a distraction to students who come in and out of her office. If asked, report that you don't like dogs, but that you make an exception for the school security dog. You never use Post-it notes. (You hate sticky things.) Instead, you file everything. During first and second periods, you monitor the halls. You always use black, blue, or red pens. You have a hairdresser whose name is Shirley.

Suspect C

(School Security Guard, Dog Owner)

You have access to the entire building. You are always serious, so you think those pigs are silly. Frequently, you make fun of the secretary because she talks to her pigs and straightens them when she should be doing her job. You love your dog and play jokes on those who don't love your dog as much as you do. (But you don't disclose this information.) Just continue to make comments about the pig disappearing, and tease Suspect A. If asked, report that you use Post-it notes for everything. During second period, you monitor halls and frequently roam in and out of the east and west offices. You always use a black pen. Your dog groomer's name is Shirley. If specifically asked, reveal that you have a 6:00 PM grooming appointment for the dog.

Suspect D

(Records Secretary)

You have access to the east office. Since you collect angels, you admire the secretary's pig collection. Make several comments about the amount of people that come in and out of the office every day. Mention that you believe any number of people could have taken that pig: students, parents, teachers, custodians, or security personnel. If asked, admit that you do not like dogs because they smell and because a stray dog bit you when you were a kid. You use Post-it notes on everything! During first and second period, you were on the phone except for a break when you used the restroom near the east office. You always use a pencil or blue pen and a highlighter. You have a daughter-in-law named Shirley.

Suspect E

(School Counselor, Niagara Falls Trip Chaperone)

You like pigs. You found a pig in an empty office with a Post-it note lying on the floor that said, "Remind self: 6:00 PM with Shirley." Having heard about the missing pig, you report this incident to the CSI class immediately. You mention the Post-it note found on the floor, explaining that you left that note untouched. You also report that you overheard Suspect F talking and laughing about the pig to someone on the phone. You think Suspect F is guilty, as she wants to be in the east office, not the west. You know she would do anything to get Suspect A to retire so she could slip into her position. If asked, explain that you use whatever writing utensil is within reach. Your great aunt's name was Shirley, but she is no longer living.

Suspect F

(Attendance Secretary)

You have access to the east office. You want that secretary's job. You think you would like it better than yours, because she gets to interact more with students. Furthermore, you have friends that work in the east office. You think it's funny that her pig is missing. You comment, "Maybe she will decide to retire now, and I could fill her position." If asked, report that you like dogs. You use Post-it notes frequently. Every day, you are extremely busy during first and second periods doing attendance on the computer. However, on the day of the incident, you did get up to go to the mailroom for a few minutes during that time. You always use a black pen. Your best friend's name is Shirley.

The Case of the Missing Spelling Bee Plaque

Background:

The Case of the Missing Spelling Bee Plaque was a huge success. It was centered on the plaque for our own All-school Spelling Bee. This treasure has been hanging in the building for over 25 years. Each year the winner of the All-school Spelling Bee receives many awards. His or her name and the school year are engraved on the plaque, which hangs in the library for all to see.

When the disappearance of the plaque was discovered, the librarian wasn't able to get to my classroom to report the crime. However, she called my classroom, and I put her on the speaker. Students immediately began taking notes and couldn't wait to get upstairs to the library to begin the investigation.

When I was developing the CSI details, I got some ideas by looking carefully at the spelling bee plaque. One student had won two years in a row. I changed her name to the name of a student who was a favorite of the attendance secretary. I changed another name from the past to the name of another secretary's cousin. This second secretary worked in the main office and made the daily morning announcements. She became my guilty suspect.

In the scenario, she took the plaque for her cousin, as his win was his biggest accomplishment. There was no truth to this, but it worked out great for the "crime." Another logical suspect was the school principal. His office was full of awards and plaques. Anyone who had been in his office knew this, and he immediately became a suspect.

Since the plaque was stolen from the library, this became Crime Scene A. The Security Office, where the plaque was found, became Crime Scene B. This space was easy to rope off with crime-scene tape. A note reading "Call Shawn ASAP" and some hairs were found in the library meeting room. This opened the door for students to use the textile, chromatography, and handwriting labs. It also required them to write search-warrant affidavits to obtain samples of hair, pens, and handwriting samples from suspects.

29

The Case of the Missing Spelling Bee Plaque

Roles for Victim and Suspects

Notes:

- *Each participant received a copy of the CSI Participant Information sheet and individual role description. See pages 19 and 20 for these templates.*

- *The following pages contain role descriptions given to the participants.*

Victim and Suspect A

(Librarian)

On Thursday, the All-school Spelling Bee plaque that has hung in the library for over 25 years disappeared. You are sure that the plaque was there at the beginning of first period. When you entered the library that morning, you looked at it and realized that the name of the 2008 winner had not been added to the plaque. You wrote a note to yourself to get this done right away.

During first period, you ran some errands in the building. You returned at the end of that period, noticed the reminder note you had written, and went to get the plaque. But it was gone! You looked everywhere, to no avail. You asked everyone whom you thought could possibly have taken it for any logical reason. When you finally decided that it must have been stolen, you reported this to the CSI class. By the way, though you know some individuals who are named Shawn, there is no reason you would place a call to any of them.

Suspect B

(School Special Education Coordinator)

You have access to every room in the building. You don't teach a class first period, but you are usually out of your office checking on your caseload of 100 students. You overheard Suspect C (the Attendance Secretary) on the phone saying, "I should just go get the Spelling Bee plaque from the library." When investigators question you, tell them, "I think she took it because she wanted to give it to her favorite former student, Fionna Jemison. Fionna won the spelling bee two years in a row and she probably wants to hang the plaque on her wall." Continue to tell students how the secretary was so proud of Fionna. Your boyfriend's name is Shawn.

Suspect C

(Attendance Secretary)

You have access to the library. During first period, you are busy with daily attendance and sometimes deliver mail to the staff mailroom. You made a comment to the librarian that the name of the 2008 spelling bee should be added to the plaque before school closes for the summer. Suspect B overheard you on the phone telling someone that you're considering getting the plaque engraved yourself because you know how busy the librarian is. Tell investigators that you know some of the students on the plaque and any one of them might have taken the plaque to hang it on their wall. Say, "If that plaque contained my name, I would want it on my wall." Continue to tell students that one of your former favorite students, Fionna Jemison, was a winner two years in a row back in 2000 and 2001. Tell them how proud you are of her and how sure you are that she would love to have that plaque hanging on her wall. Your son's name is Shawn.

sample CSI scenario 3

Suspect D

(Principal)

You have access to every room in the building at all times. During first period, you monitor the halls, run errands in the building, and check all the bathrooms. You have many plaques in your office. You believe that all awards and achievement plaques should be hung in your office, as you like to admire the achievements of your students. You think that the All-school Spelling Bee Plaque should hang in your office, but you respect the librarian's wish to keep it in the library where it has been for 25 years. You know many people named Shawn.

Suspect E

(School Security Officer)

You have access to every room in the building at all times. During first period, you monitor the halls and check doors. You went into an empty meeting room to interview a student about some bathroom graffiti. That is when you saw the plaque on the table. Remembering the rumors going around the school about the missing spelling bee plaque, you decided to leave the room immediately. You left everything untouched and reported it to the CSI class. You know many people named Shawn.

Suspect F

(Secretary in the Main Office)

You have access to every room in the building during school hours. After morning announcements, you run errands around the building. Tell investigators, "I know some of the people on that plaque. My cousin was a winner back in 1989. We were so proud of him. I should have been on that plaque too, but you know how it is. Yes, the family was so proud, they threw a big party for him after the big win. Yes, I should have been on that plaque." (Don't tell students your cousin's name unless they specifically ask.)

Shhh! You are guilty! You took the plaque because your cousin, Shawn Kent, was the 1989 winner and it's been his only great accomplishment. You know that he would love to have it hanging on his wall.

Getting Ready for CSI

CRIME SCENE DO NOT CROSS CRIME SCENE DO NOT CROSS

CSI at a Glance

Planning & Preparation:
Do these before the CSI begins.

Scenario: Plan a crime scenario within your building.
Pattern your unit after one of the sample scenarios from real classrooms, or create your own idea. Use the many planning guidelines and templates provided.

Suspects: Line up some victims and suspects to take part.
Find people in the school who will agree to participate. Give each volunteer a role and the details of the scenario.

Fingerprints: Collect fingerprints from victims and suspects.
Follow the instructions for fingerprinting suspects and victims to prepare a Fingerprint Template for each one. Collect fingerprints of the guilty suspect on several evidence tags.

Crime Scene(s): Find locations for the crime scenes.
There may be one or two scenes. They need to be spaces in the school that can be roped off and untouched for a week or two. Make arrangements to use these spaces.

Evidence: Gather and prepare evidence.
Collect all items that will be left at the scene of the crime. In addition to objects, this may include bite impressions, notes written by the guilty suspect (or other suspects), and ink pens.

Team Folders: Prepare a folder for each team.
Use the team folder instructions to get folders ready. Place necessary sheets and forms in the folders. Get two small notebooks or pads for each CSI team. Put these in the folders.

Police and ID Badges: Prepare these two kinds of badges.
Follow directions on the CSI Police Badge Lanyard teacher page to make 6 to 8 badges on necklaces. Take (or get) wallet-sized pictures of all students. Follow instructions on the CSI ID Badge teacher page to make individual ID badges.

Cameras: Get prepared to photograph the crime scenes.
Find one or more digital cameras for photographing the crime scene(s). Plan a system for downloading and printing the photos. Follow the instructions for mounting photos.

CSI Kits: Prepare CSI kits.
Gather all the supplies that students will need for collecting evidence and investigating the crime scene.

CSI Forms: Be prepared with all the forms for the CSI.
Make copies of all forms, worksheets, templates, and lab sheets that students will need. Pay special attention to the CSI Readiness Checklist.

Forensic Lab: Set up the classroom forensic lab.
Reserve an area in your classroom for the forensic science lab. Include a table, lab equipment, and supplies for use in analyzing evidence. See the master list of supplies that accompanies the prelabs.

Prelabs:
Complete these with students before the CSI begins.

Observations & Inferences:
Sharpen skills needed to make good observations and evidence-based inferences.

Fingerprints:
Take fingerprints, learn fingerprint types, and gain experience examining and comparing fingerprints. A parent permission slip is required for this lab, and is included.

Bite Impressions:
Contribute, examine, compare, and analyze teeth impressions.

Handwriting:
Observe, compare, and analyze types of handwriting.

Mystery Powders:
Test and identify mystery substances, examining their chemical and physical reactions with certain liquids.

Chromatography:
Learn a method for examining and comparing different ink pigments found in pens or markers.

Textiles:
Practice using a microscope to observe the properties and characteristics of different types of textiles.

The CSI begins!

Set up the crime scene(s) *in time for the day when the crime is discovered and you are ready for the investigation to begin.*

Review roles and procedures *with the volunteer victims and suspects.*

Assign students to CSI teams *of four or five. Give teams time to choose names, read about jobs, and select jobs.*

Introduce team folders *and explain their purpose and use.*

Show off the CSI kits, *introducing students to supplies. Explain how, where, and when to use them.*

Introduce the forensic science lab *by showing students where it is and what is in it. Review procedures for its use.*

Explain the procedures *for*
> *– leaving the classroom to investigate*
> *– photographing, handling, and tagging evidence*
> *– getting, handling, and examining fingerprints and bite impressions*
> *– using the police badges and individual photo ID badges*
> *– obtaining and using search warrants*
> *– interviewing suspects and keeping records*

Explain the reports *due from the CSI Team.*

Introduce the CSI Scoring Rubric *and other assessment forms.*

The CSI begins with the report of the crime!

Students are prepared and eager *to leave the classroom to investigate the crime scene, obtain evidence, examine evidence in the lab, film news broadcasts, write search warrants, interview suspects, and write formal reports.*

The CSI ends.

Teams draw conclusions, *then write and present final reports.*

Students assess *the teams, their own performances, and the CSI.*

The CSI is shared and celebrated. *Find a way to wrap up, share results, and celebrate a job well done!*

 CSI Bulletin Board Ideas

Create a great bulletin board to excite the students and kick off the CSI experience! Here are some suggestions for bulletin board elements.

Directions:

1. Get some bright yellow "Police Line Do Not Cross" tape, "Crime Scene Do Not Cross" tape, or "Caution" tape. Visit party supply stores, a hardware store, your local police department, or the Internet to find this. Your custodian may have some yellow "Caution" tape.

2. Find, buy, make, or borrow police hats, plastic police or sheriff badges, magnifying glasses, footprint dye cuts, wanted posters, CSI movie or TV memorabilia, evidence tape, evidence folders, evidence tags, police patches, police batons, police radios, or handcuffs. Use any police artifacts.

Other Suggestions:

- *Visit your local police department. Ask for anything they may have to help you with this project (such as evidence tags, evidence tape, police tape, old hats, or police department patches).*

- *Arrange for a police officer or detective to visit your classroom and share the profession with your students. Specifically ask for an officer to demonstrate how to dust for and preserve fingerprint evidence.*

- *If your local police department is easily accessible, plan a field trip to tour it.*

CSI in the Classroom

CSI Team Folders

Team folders are used to keep all team materials together. This can be a file folder or any other folder you choose.

Directions:

1. Get one folder for each CSI team and make copies of the team folder template on page 39.

2. Prepare the folders. Cut out templates and glue them to the front covers of the folders. Insert materials into the folders. (See list below.)

3. Set up a designated box or bin for team folders.

4. Have teams choose one member from each to be responsible for the folder every day.

5. Before passing out folders to teams, explain the purpose of the folder. Review all of the items that should be kept in the folder.

Place these in each folder:

- CSI Job Description & Sign-up Sheet
- List of CSI Team Reports
- CSI Scoring Rubric and Information sheet
- Forensic Science Terminology Worksheet
- Activity Log (one for each team member)
- Mounting Photos, Instructions
- Suspect List
- Evidence List
- Police Chief Public News Broadcast Form
- Ink Analysis Worksheet
- CSI Team Review and CSI Reflection

Explanation to Give to Students:

Team folders are used to keep all CSI materials together in one place. In addition to the materials initially in the folder, everything else that is used or developed should be added. This includes: reports, photos, scale drawings, interview notes, mininotebooks, evidence tags, search warrants and affidavits, ID badges, and anything else that relates to the CSI.

CSI Team Folder

Team Name

_____

Team Members

_____

_____

_____

_____

_____

✔ Pick up your team folder each day and return it before you leave.

✔ Be sure to keep all CSI materials in this folder.

✔ Don't forget to log your daily activities on your individual Activity Logs.

✔ Remember to put all team members' names on every assignment.

✔ All written materials must be proofread, edited, and revised in your best handwriting or typed in 12-point font and double-spaced before submission.

✔ This is a group effort. Teamwork is the key to your success!

CSI Kit

Prepare for each CSI team a kit like the ones police officers and detectives would use to look for and gather evidence. Put supplies and tools into some sort of carrier or plastic bag for easy transport to the crime scene or to any other secondary scenes or places where the team might secure further evidence. Include all items that they will need to do their jobs.

CAMERA

MAGNIFYING GLASSES

TWEEZERS

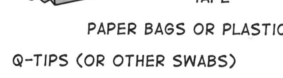

RUBBER GLOVES

TEAM NOTEBOOKS

MEASURING TOOLS

BRUSHES AND FINGERPRINT POWDER

TAPE

PAPER BAGS OR PLASTIC BAGS

Q-TIPS (OR OTHER SWABS)

SMALL BOTTLES (TO COLLECT SUBSTANCES)

SPOON OR EYEDROPPER

WRITING AND DRAWING IMPLEMENTS

GRAPH PAPER

EVIDENCE TAGS

CRIME-SCENE TAPE

Students must take police badges and ID badges every time they leave the classroom to do CSI work.

Back in the Classroom:

Students label all evidence with evidence tags, then log it on the Evidence List and discuss (in teams) what the evidence reveals. They will have other tools and supplies there in the forensic lab where the scientists will examine evidence further.

CSI Police Badge Lanyards

The visible police badge serves as a pass for students to be out of the classroom and allows suspects to change into their CSI participation roles when they see students approach. The police badges also limit to eight or fewer the number of students exiting your classroom, since a student must wear one around the neck when leaving the classroom for CSI business. When introducing CSI procedures, emphasize the necessity of wearing this lanyard when leaving the classroom. Also, read aloud to your class the information on the back of each badge. Discuss this with students.

Directions:

1. Purchase six to eight inexpensive **police** or **sheriff badges** from a discount store, dollar store, or party supply store. Or make your own badges.

2. Glue each badge on a rectangular piece of black cardstock or heavy construction paper as shown. Attach a lanyard or a long piece of string or yarn to each top corner of the card stock. Make sure this is long enough to pull over the head easily.

3. Make passes using the templates on page 44. Fill in the teacher's name on the passes. Glue a pass to the back of the cardstock.

Note: If time permits, involve students in making badges in preparation for an upcoming CSI. Enlist parent volunteers to help, if needed.

CSI Identification Badges

Each student needs an individual ID badge for the CSI experience. This badge serves three purposes: it serves as a pass, it offers identification to your suspects and victim(s) that might not know a student, and it makes the experience more fun and realistic for the students. When introducing CSI procedures, explain to students the need to take this ID badge when leaving the classroom to investigate. Also, review with students the pass on the back of each badge.

front cover

Directions:

1. Start with a piece of 9 by 12-inch black cardstock or heavy construction paper. Fold the paper in half (lengthwise, landscape orientation) and cut it into three equal pieces. This gives three wallet-like badges that, when unfolded, measure nine by four inches.

2. Make copies of these templates found on pages 43 and 44: CSI ID Badge Template, CSI Task Force Label, CSI Investigator Label, and CSI Pass.

3. Glue a CSI badge image to the front of each wallet. Glue one pass to the back of each badge.
   Note: Remember to add the teacher's name to the pass.

   4. On the inside, glue a wallet-sized photo of the student to the upper flap. Glue a CSI investigator label and a task force label to the inside bottom as shown. Students will fill in information needed for the task force label on Day One of the CSI, after they have chosen team names and jobs.

   Note: If time permits, involve students in making badges in preparation for an upcoming CSI! Enlist parent volunteers to help if needed.

inside

back

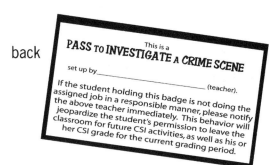

PASS TO INVESTIGATE A CRIME SCENE
This is a

set up by_____
_____ (teacher).

If the student holding this badge is not doing the assigned job in a responsible manner, please notify the above teacher immediately. This behavior will jeopardize the student's permission to leave the classroom for future CSI activities, as well as his or her CSI grade for the current grading period.

CSI Badge Templates (for use on individual ID badges)

Cut and paste
CSI Badge Template (#1) to the
front of the folded CSI badge.

1. **CSI** Badge Template

Cut and paste labels #2 and #3
to the **bottom inside** half of the **CSI** badge.

Crime Investigator: _____

TASK FORCE

Team:_____

Job: _____

2. **CSI** Task Force Template

CSI INVESTIGATOR

3. **CSI** Investigator Label Template

....

CSI Badge Templates (for use on individual ID badges)

Cut and paste
CSI Badge Template (#1) to the
front of the folded CSI badge.

1. **CSI** Badge Template

Cut and paste labels #2 and #3
to the **bottom inside** half of the **CSI** badge.

Crime Investigator: _____

TASK FORCE

Team:_____

Job: _____

2. **CSI** Task Force Template

CSI INVESTIGATOR

3. **CSI** Investigator Label Template

CSI in the Classroom

CSI Pass Templates

(for use on police badges and individual ID badges)

This is a
PASS TO INVESTIGATE A CRIME SCENE

set up by_____ (teacher).

If the student holding this badge is not doing the assigned job in a responsible manner, please notify the above teacher immediately. This behavior will jeopardize the student's permission to leave the classroom for future CSI activities, as well as his or her CSI grade for the current grading period.

This is a
PASS TO INVESTIGATE A CRIME SCENE

set up by_____ (teacher).

If the student holding this badge is not doing the assigned job in a responsible manner, please notify the above teacher immediately. This behavior will jeopardize the student's permission to leave the classroom for future CSI activities, as well as his or her CSI grade for the current grading period.

This is a
PASS TO INVESTIGATE A CRIME SCENE

set up by_____ (teacher).

If the student holding this badge is not doing the assigned job in a responsible manner, please notify the above teacher immediately. This behavior will jeopardize the student's permission to leave the classroom for future CSI activities, as well as his or her CSI grade for the current grading period.

This is a
PASS TO INVESTIGATE A CRIME SCENE

set up by_____ (teacher).

If the student holding this badge is not doing the assigned job in a responsible manner, please notify the above teacher immediately. This behavior will jeopardize the student's permission to leave the classroom for future CSI activities, as well as his or her CSI grade for the current grading period.

This is a
PASS TO INVESTIGATE A CRIME SCENE

set up by_____ (teacher).

If the student holding this badge is not doing the assigned job in a responsible manner, please notify the above teacher immediately. This behavior will jeopardize the student's permission to leave the classroom for future CSI activities, as well as his or her CSI grade for the current grading period.

This is a
PASS TO INVESTIGATE A CRIME SCENE

set up by_____ (teacher).

If the student holding this badge is not doing the assigned job in a responsible manner, please notify the above teacher immediately. This behavior will jeopardize the student's permission to leave the classroom for future CSI activities, as well as his or her CSI grade for the current grading period.

Fingerprinting the Suspects

Fingerprints are often found at a crime scene. The body produces natural oils and sweat, creating a perfect medium with which to leave fingerprints on any object or surface touched. Prints can be found on door handles, windows, glass, and other smooth objects or surfaces. Each individual has a unique pattern for all of the fingers, and no two persons' fingerprints are alike. Since a fingerprint will remain unchanged for the entire life of the individual, any one person will have only one set of prints. Thus prints are useful in placing suspects at the scene of a crime.

Fingerprints found on an object or surface are called **latent** prints. These are the invisible (or barely visible) prints that must be developed through the use of dusting powder or a chemical solution. Prints taken directly from a person's fingers through the use of ink are referred to as **inked** prints.

Fingerprint the suspects before the CSI begins.

During the CSI, the process of fingerprinting victims and suspects becomes complicated. There will be several CSI teams in each class—all wanting to get fingerprints from each suspect. This would mean fingerprinting each suspect several times, and doing so under hurried conditions. The prints are often inaccurate, and the process of being fingerprinted by several teams burdens the volunteers. So it is recommended that you obtain fingerprints ahead of time from the staff members who have agreed to participate in the CSI.

Make some fingerprint evidence tags ahead of time.

Evidence tags keep a record of fingerprints that are found during an investigation. You can encourage students to collect this information from the crime scenes. They will want to try this. However, this is an inexact science. So a backup plan is wise. In case students have a difficult time lifting accurate prints at the crime scene, it is a good idea to have real fingerprints from the actual guilty suspect already on some evidence tags.

Arrange for clear prints at the crime scenes.

When you set up the crime scenes, make sure that items and surfaces in the scene are clean of random fingerprints. Try to get fresh prints from the actual suspects ONTO the evidence at the scene. In addition, you could add other fingerprints from anyone else who had a reason (legitimate or not) to be there.

Directions for fingerprinting suspects:

1. Review the procedure for taking inked prints. You'll find this on the lab page for Fingerprint Prelab, Part I (page 105).

2. Make enough copies of the Fingerprint Template (page 47) for all your suspects and the victims. (Always assume that a victim is also a suspect.) Write the guilty suspect's name on one, and the names of the other suspects on the others.

3. Get the fingerprints long before you begin the CSI. Make a copy of each template after the prints are collected.

4. Keep all completed fingerprint templates (and copies) in a secure place in the classroom.

5. When students present you with a satisfactory search warrant affidavit for the fingerprint template of any suspect, you may approve a search warrant and loan them the template.

6. All suspect fingerprint templates must be returned to you at the end of each class period. No template should be stored in a team folder. You will need these for other teams.

Directions for fingerprint evidence tags:

1. Make several copies of the Fingerprint Evidence Tag Template on page 48.

2. Prepare a tag with a fingerprint from the guilty suspect for any piece of evidence or crime scene location where you will place that suspect's prints.

3. Complete each tag with all the necessary information. Make copies of the tags.

3. Keep these tags (and copies) in a secure place in the classroom.

4. When students present you with a satisfactory search warrant affidavit for prints from the crime scene or any piece of evidence, you may approve a search warrant and loan them an evidence tag.

Note: Always assume that a victim (or one who reports the crime) is also a suspect.

Victim or Suspect _____

CSI Fingerprint Template for Suspects

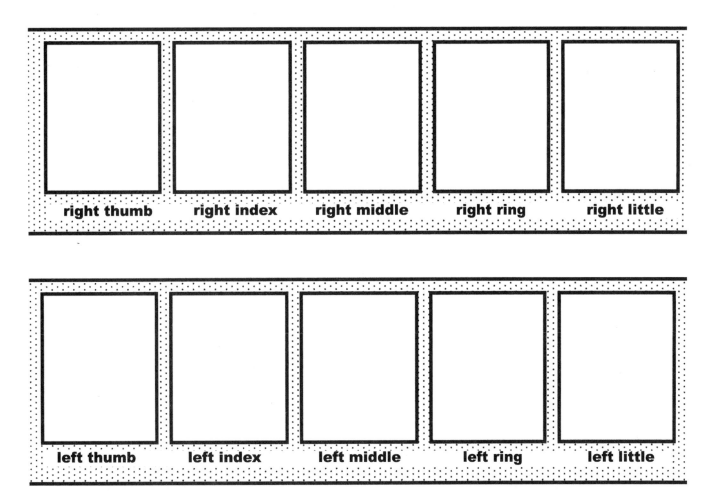

| right thumb | right index | right middle | right ring | right little |

| left thumb | left index | left middle | left ring | left little |

CSI INVESTIGATORS:

Use this sheet as a reference for comparing fingerprints to those found during CSI investigations.

Please do not write on this sheet.

Return this to your teacher as soon as you are done using it.

DO NOT put it into your team folder.

Thank you

CSI in the Classroom

CSI Fingerprint Evidence Tag Template

(Note to teacher: Make three tags with fingerprints matching the guilty suspect.)

Evidence Tag for Fingerprints

Print Taken From _____

Date _____

Obtained By _____

Location (Crime Scene): _____

Who do you think is the owner of this print? _____

Write a written report explaining your results. Include all of the information from this evidence tag.

Evidence Tag for Fingerprints

Print Taken From _____

Date _____

Obtained By _____

Location (Crime Scene): _____

Who do you think is the owner of this print? _____

Write a written report explaining your results. Include all of the information from this evidence tag.

Evidence Tag for Fingerprints

Print Taken From _____

Date _____

Obtained By _____

Location (Crime Scene): _____

Who do you think is the owner of this print? _____

Write a written report explaining your results. Include all of the information from this evidence tag.

 Forensic Lab

The forensic lab is an area in the classroom that provides students with materials for all of the prelabs that relate to your CSI. This lab needs a table or other ample surface space. It is a place where students will bring evidence and examine it carefully. There must be space for all necessary supplies.

Preparing the Forensic Lab:

1. Use a cardboard folding divider to partition off the lab area.

2. Set out only the equipment and substances that are safe. Substances such as vinegar, iodine solution, sharp tools, or small tools (easily lost) should be kept out of reach until needed.

3. Refer to the lists of materials used for the prelabs on page 100. Collect in this lab only the things your students will need, based on the kinds of evidence you have planted at the crime scenes. For instance, if you don't include any mystery substances in your CSI, then you will not need supplies for that lab.

4. Don't assist students with the case by telling them what lab processes they need to pursue. Instead, remind them that they have the prior knowledge of the prelabs that you did together in class. They also have the lab sheets from those prelabs for reference. It is the job of the team to decide what they need to do in order to solve the case.

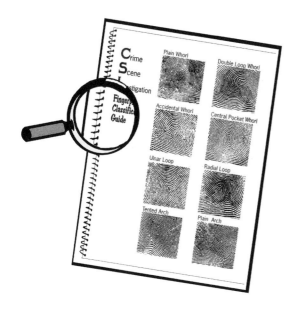

Note: Only the forensic scientist(s) from each team may enter the forensic lab to obtain or borrow equipment. The police chief may assist, but others should not enter or borrow anything from the lab area. The forensic scientists are responsible for all materials and the daily cleanup and organization of the lab.

49

Readiness Checklist

If you've got these things complete and under control, you are ready!

____Create your CSI scenario plan (including crime scene sketches).

____Review the CSI Daily Agenda.

____Plan your own schedule and daily agenda.

____Complete all necessary prelabs with students.

____Make police badge lanyards and individual ID badges.

____Prepare CSI team folders.

____Prepare CSI kits for teams.

____Give job role descriptions to victim and suspects.

____Take fingerprints from victim(s) and suspects. (Use fingerprint templates.)

____Get fingerprints of guilty suspect(s) on several fingerprint evidence tags.

____If needed, take bite impressions from appropriate suspects.

____If a written sample is used, distribute pens to suspects.

____If a written sample is used, get copies of this written by the appropriate suspect.

____Gather all supplies needed to set up crime scenes.

Make copies of all forms needed:

   ____Any needed lab sheets or forms from prelabs

   ____Search Warrant Affidavit and Approved Search Warrant

   ____Evidence Tags

   ____Fingerprint Template and Fingerprint Classification Guide

   ____Job Descriptions & Sign-up sheet

   ____List of CSI Team Reports and Final Report Outline

   ____Police Chief Public Information Broadcast form

   ____CSI Scoring Rubric and Team Information sheet

   ____Forensic Science Terminology Worksheet

   ____Activity Log

   ____Mounting Photos Team Information sheet

   ____Suspect List

   ____Evidence List

   ____CSI Pen Analysis Worksheet

   ____Team Review and CSI Reflection

____Set out a supply of Search Warrant Affidavits and evidence tags.

____Get graph paper for scale drawings.

____Get a digital camera, computer, printer, and materials for mounting photos.

CSI Begins

CRIME SCENE DO NOT CROSS CRIME SCENE DO NOT CRO

CRIME SCENE DO NOT CROSS CRIME SCENE DO NOT CRO

CSI Daily Agenda
Job Descriptions & Sign-up Sheet
CSI Team Reports
CSI Scoring Rubric
CSI Terminology
Activity Log
Mounting Photos
Scale Drawings
Suspect List
Search Warrants
Evidence List
Evidence Tags
Police Chief Public News Broadcast
Chromatography During the CSI

CSI Daily Agenda

Objectives for Day One:

- Explain uses and procedures for team folders, job descriptions, police badge lanyards, and ID badges.
- Form CSI teams and choose team names.
- Choose CSI jobs.
- Complete ID badges.

Activities to do today:

For management purposes, it is crucial to explain the folders, jobs, and both badges before students move into CSI teams for the first time.

1. Introduce students to the first day of the CSI. Let them know that they will form and work in teams. Stress the importance of keeping all CSI team information top secret!

2. Show students the team folder and explain how it is used. Read through the labels on the team folder. Explain that they will work together as a team to decide on a team name. All team members' names should be written on the nameplate on the front of the folder.

3. Read through the Job Descriptions sheet. Explain that each person will sign up for only one job. This sheet allows students to understand what each job entails before they commit to one.

4. Explain the police badge lanyards and procedures for using them.

5. Show students an ID badge and describe the purpose. Explain that they will complete the ID badges after they have chosen jobs.

6. Before students move into teams, give students time to ask questions. Be sure all their questions are answered.

7. Now students can move into teams. Pass out ID badges and team folders.

8. Give students time to decide on a team name, sign up for jobs, and complete their ID badges.

9. Each team should appoint one member to be responsible for the team folder every day. They can put a star next to that name on the nameplate. Let students know where folders are to be left each day.

CSI Daily Agenda

CSI DAY 2

Objectives for Day Two:

- Review procedures learned on Day One.
- Understand reports that teams are responsible for.
- Review and understand rubrics for CSI assessment.
- Learn how to use Activity Logs.
- Bring Activity Logs up to date.

Activities to do today:

1. Review all of the procedures discussed on Day One.

2. Introduce students to the list of CSI team reports. Explain the team responsibilities for all these written reports. Encourage them to become familiar with this list.

3. Instruct students to keep the list of CSI reports in the team folder at all times. As each report is prepared, it must be labeled and kept in the team folder.

4. Read and explain the CSI Scoring Rubric, the Team Review, and the CSI Reflection. Go through them carefully and answer student questions.

5. Examine the Activity Log sheets together. The team folder should contain one for each student. Students should fill in their names and the team names on these logs. Explain the purpose of this sheet.

6. Guide students in completing the first two sections of the Activity Log to record what they have done on Day One and Day Two of the CSI unit. On Day One, they formed teams, decided on team names, learned about the different CSI jobs, signed up for jobs, completed ID badges, and learned procedures for folders, police badge lanyards, and ID badges. On Day Two, they learned about the required CSI reports and procedures for use of the Activity Log.

7. To end Day Two of the CSI, instruct students to keep the list of reports, rubrics, and log sheets in the team folder. The students who took responsibility for collecting folders should put folders away in the appropriate place.

CSI Daily Agenda

Objectives for Day Three:

- Review procedures for keeping Activity Logs.
- Understand reasons for requesting search warrants.
- Learn procedures for obtaining search warrants.
- Learn how to complete a search warrant affidavit.
- Learn procedures for using evidence tags.
- Bring Activity Logs up to date.

Activities to do today:

1. Begin with a quick review of the Activity Log procedures.

2. Give each student a copy of a search warrant affidavit. Show students where these forms are located in the classroom.

3. Explain the purpose of the affidavits. (Refer to pages 81–83 for information.) Make it clear that they must write a search warrant affidavit any time they request fingerprints or any items (such as a pen, clothing sample, bite sample, or shoe print) from a suspect or any other individual.

4. Discuss the concept of probable cause. Give examples of situations in which there is or is not probable cause for requesting something from a suspect. Make sure students know how to fill out this section of the search warrant affidavit.

5. Explain that, in order to obtain a handwriting sample, teeth impressions, or other items from a suspect, students must also get an approved search warrant. When they ask a suspect or anyone else for these samples, they must show the approved search warrant to that person.

6. Explain also that the teacher keeps the fingerprint template and ink pen for each suspect. The teacher will loan these to CSI team members when a search warrant has been approved.

7. Explain the procedures for using evidence tags for fingerprints and artifacts. Provide copies of the evidence tags. Show students where they are located in the classroom.

8. Remind students to fill in their Activity Logs for the day, and put them back in the team folder.

CSI Daily Agenda

CSI DAY
4

Objectives for Day Four:

- Hear the report of the crime.

- Prepare questions to ask the victim (complainant).

- Interview the victim.

- Receive instructions for the first steps in the out-of-the classroom investigation.

- Prepare first public news broadcast (police chief).

- Bring Activity Logs up to date.

Activities to do today:

1. Before long, Day Four of the CSI will become quite exciting. But to begin, pass out a sheet of lined paper to every member of each team.

2. Tell students that you will review procedures for search warrants and evidence tags, and that they should use this paper to take notes.

3. Begin conducting your review. Shortly, you will be interrupted by a (preplanned) phone call or a visit from a victim who comes rushing into your classroom. The victim will make a report about a crime. It is important that all students have the paper ready for taking notes, as the victim (person bringing a complaint) will only have a few minutes to make the initial report.

4. Students may ask a few questions of the victim. The victim's testimony should reveal what happened, when, and where, if possible.

5. After the victim finishes the initial report, students will be excited and want to start discussing their thoughts within their teams. Give them a few minutes to talk about it and encourage them to come up with some questions for the victim (person making the complaint).

6. When students begin asking if they can go find the victim to ask more questions, then you are ready to continue. Ask for their attention and explain that you need to give them more information before they leave to visit the crime scene.

Day Four Agenda continues on next page.

7. Send the police officers from all teams to the crime scene to secure it with crime-scene tape. Instruct them to secure the scene without touching anything, then to return immediately to the classroom.

8. Explain to students that the police officer(s) on each team will go to the crime scene where the victim noticed the problem and begin the investigation. Before anyone is allowed to leave the classroom, she or he must have at least three to five questions written out and ready for the victim.

9. Explain to students that police officers will take pictures of the area in which the crime occurred. Those pictures will be mounted on construction paper or poster paper and labeled "Crime Scene A" with explanatory captions under each picture. Be sure to explain how to take, develop, and mount the photos. Use a computer and printer to print out copies of the photos. Ask teams to review the instruction sheet for mounting photos. The photos must be presented as if they were to be used as evidence in a courtroom.

TOP SECRET

10. Explain that the forensic scientist is responsible for a scale drawing or three-dimensional model of the crime scene. Provide graph paper to each team for the scale drawing. The drawing or model should include a key and should be labeled "Crime Scene A." It is to be prepared and presented as if it were evidence to be used in a courtroom.

11. If a video camera is available, plan for the police chief on each team to prepare a public news broadcast. The broadcast is based on information that the team has gathered in the investigation so far. Provide Police Chief Public News Broadcast forms for each team. The broadcast is to be written, practiced, and presented in front of a video camera. If a camera is NOT available, the police chief can write the report and present it over the PA system or in an email or wherever possible.

12. Remind students to fill in Activity Logs and put them back in the team folder along with their notes, the scale drawings, sheets of photos, and the Police Chiefs News Public News Broadcast forms.

Note: It is likely that much of your time in this class period will be used by the initial review, the victim's visit, the questions, and your further instructions. So out-of-the-classroom investigation will probably be best left until the next day of the CSI. However, if there is plenty of time after the above activities, you can begin on the Day Five Agenda.

CSI Daily Agenda

CSI DAY 5

Objectives for Day Five:

- Review information gained from the victim.
- Create questions for interviewing the victim.
- Visit Crime Scene A, gather clues, take notes, and interview the victim and witnesses.
- Photograph Crime Scene A; then print, mount, and label photographs.
- Take measurements at Crime Scene A and make rough scale drawings or plans for a model of the scene.
- Begin a Suspect List.
- Learn some CSI terminology and do Internet research about forensic science.
- Work on investigation reports and scale drawings or models of Crime Scene A.
- Bring Activity Logs up to date.

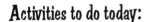

Activities to do today:

Day Four was exciting! The scenario has actually begun, and students are enthusiastic and ready to dive in. Day Five and beyond will get even busier. Make sure that students are clear on all procedures and protocol. This is very important for a well-run CSI and for classroom management.

1. Review the information given to the class by the victim. Encourage students to start thinking about who might be suspects and who could be interviewed for more information.

2. The police officers spring into action on this day as they go to investigate the Crime Scene A. Once there, they will ask questions and take photos. (You may choose to send the police chief from each team along to assist if there is not a second police officer.)

3. The forensic scientists also visit the crime scene to take measurements in preparation for designing a scale drawing or model of the crime scene.

4. Remember that police officers do not leave the classroom to interview anyone without questions written in the spiral notebook. Team members can work together to create these questions before the police officers leave the classroom. The police chief should review and approve these questions.

Day Five Agenda continues on next page.

5. Each police officer or scientist leaving the room must take a police badge lanyard and the individual ID. (Remember to limit the number of students out of your classroom at a time.) Investigators will need to take their CSI kits.

6. If a digital camera is available, students will have to share it and rotate it during their investigation. You may have to limit each group's time out of the classroom to ten minutes, so that each team has time to get photographs.

7. The students remaining in the classroom should be referred to the Suspect List in their ream folders. Ask them to think about, discuss, and list a few suspects who they think may be involved, given the information received the previous day.

8. Students can also work on the CSI Terminology Worksheets.

9. If computers with web access are available, students can begin to explore forensic science activities and information on the Internet. See the Excellent Websites for CSI list on page 127.

10. When the police officers and scientists return, they should share with their teams the information gathered. The whole team can work together to complete the Investigation Report, using the list of CSI Team Reports and the CSI Scoring Rubric as guides.

11. When all photographs of Crime Scene A have been taken, these can be downloaded into the computer and printed. Teams can work together to complete the final scale drawing or three-dimensional model for Crime Scene A, mount the photos, and write captions for the photos.

12. At the end of the time for Day Five, remind students to fill in their Activity Logs and put them back in the team folders These also must be returned to the team folders: Investigation Reports, rubrics, mini-spiral notebooks, CSI Terminology Worksheets, Suspect Sheet, scale drawings or model designs, mounted photos, notes taken from Internet sites, ID badges, and any other materials used for the CSI activities of the day.

CSI Daily Agenda

Objectives for Day Six:

- Learn new information about the crime from visitor.
- Review information gained from the victim.
- Visit Crime Scene B, gather clues, and take notes.
- Photograph Crime Scene B; then print, mount, and label photographs.
- Take measurements at Crime Scene B and make rough scale drawings of the scene.
- Continue work on forensic terms, Investigation Reports, and the scale drawing from Crime Scene B.
- Expand the Suspect List, develop more questions to ask suspects, and continue interviewing suspects.
- Begin analysis of evidence and complete Crime Lab Evidence Reports.
- Complete Recovered Evidence Reports.
- Bring Activity Logs up to date.

Activities to do today:

If all CSI Teams have had a chance to investigate Crime Scene A, you're ready for the next surprise in the CSI. If not, delay these agenda items until after the last team has returned to the classroom, or until the next day.

1. The excitement of the CSI builds with a visit to the classroom (or a call) by someone with more information about the crime. This person believes he or she has found the stolen object or some other important clues left behind in a new location. (This becomes Crime Scene B.)

2. Give students time to ask a few questions of the visitor or caller and take notes. Also, give them time in their teams to prepare questions for the detectives to ask victims, suspects, witnesses, or others when they leave to investigate Crime Scene B.

Day Six Agenda continues on next page.

CSI in the Classroom

3. Send the police officers from all teams to the crime scene to secure it with crime-scene tape. Then, detectives from each team will investigate Crime Scene B to photograph the scene and ask questions. The forensic scientist will accompany the detective in order to take measurements and begin a scale drawing of Crime Scene B. Remember to limit the number of students out of the classroom at one time, and to limit the time so that all teams can visit the crime scene. If there is only one detective on the team, the police chief may assist.

4. Students remaining in the classroom can work with their teams to expand the Suspect List, based on the new information. Team members can also continue to work on the CSI Terminology Worksheet, Internet research, and the Investigation Report.

5. When the detectives return, they should share the information they gathered. The team can work to complete the Recovered Property Report.

6. Teams can also work on printing, mounting, and labeling the photos and finalizing the scale drawings for Crime Scene B.

7. As students discuss the two crime scenes and the information or evidence obtained by the police officers and detectives, they should begin to generate more questions for the victim who reported the crime and the complainant who reported finding the new information or stolen object. As they return to these two individuals, they should get information from both of them that names new suspects and reasons to interview them.

8. Teams should also begin writing questions for new suspects. When questions have been written, they can go to interview new suspects.

9. Forensic scientists should begin the process of analyzing evidence that the police officer and detectives bring to them. A Crime Lab Analysis Report must accompany each analysis of evidence.

10. At the end of the time for Day Five, remind students to fill in their Activity Logs and put them back in the team folders. These also must be returned to the team folders: Investigation Reports, rubrics, mini-spiral notebooks, CSI Terminology worksheets, Suspect Sheets, scale drawings, mounted photos, all reports and rubrics, ID badges, and any other materials used for the CSI activities of the day.

CSI Daily Agenda

CSI DAYS
7, 8, 9 ...

Objectives for Days

Seven,

Eight,

Nine, and . . . .

- Continue gaining information, analyzing evidence, and interviewing suspects, witnesses, and victims.
- Continue analysis of evidence.
- Continue discussing evidence and drawing conclusions.
- Complete evidence tags and Evidence Reports.
- Continue preparing all required reports.
- Within each team, decide the identity of the guilty party in the crime.
- Complete Final Reports.
- Give final news broadcast by the police chief.
- Bring Activity Logs up to date.

Activities to do on these days:

1. For the remainder of your CSI, Day Six activities continue and deepen. As students investigate different suspects and gain more information pertaining to the case, new suspects are identified; questions are asked; search warrants are requested for fingerprints, ink pens, fabric scraps, substances, and so on (depending upon the clues you included in your CSI scenario); evidence is analyzed; and teams continue to discuss the results of their findings.

2. Review the search warrant affidavit procedure, the meaning of probable cause, and the use of evidence tags.

3. Remind students to make additions to the Evidence Report for each item of evidence they collect, the Suspect Report description for each suspect they interview, and the Witness Report for each witness they question.

4. Remind teams that they are responsible for all the reports.

5. When most teams have come to a conclusion about the crime, advise them to use the Final Report Outline and the CSI Rubric to finish up their work. All reports should be proofread and typed or neatly written.

6. The police chief should be prepared to make a final public news broadcast to disclose all of the information collected and the apprehension of a guilty suspect(s). Use the CSI Police Chief Public News Broadcast form.

TOP SECRET

CSI in the Classroom

CSI Daily Agenda

Objectives for the Final Day:

- Present the final reports.
- Thank people who participated in the CSI.
- Identify each team's "guilty" suspect.
- Disclose the true guilty suspect.
- Complete assessments: Team Review and CSI Reflection.

Activities to do today:

1. Each team should be prepared to read the Final Report aloud.

2. If possible, invite the suspect(s) that teams have found "guilty" into the classroom to hear the reports and receive a big, "Thank you!" Invite others who participated in your CSI also. CSI participants are more likely to participate in future CSI scenarios if they know they are appreciated.

3. After each team has presented its Final Report, video news broadcasts have been played, and all team folders have been turned in, it is time for the teacher to disclose the guilty suspect(s).

4. Celebrate the winning teams. Then plan or announce plans for an event to celebrate the entire CSI.

5. Give students time to complete the Team Review and the CSI Reflection. Students should complete these assessments individually, with as much privacy as possible. The evaluations are kept confidential and used for teacher information only.

6. If there is to be a final celebration, spend some time planning or making preparations for that event.

Congratulations, teacher! You survived the CSI! Be sure to keep notes of your thoughts on the success of the varying parts, and your ideas for change. Put all of the badges and CSI artifacts away. Keep some of the best scale drawings, mounted photos, videos of news broadcasts, and reports in a folder to use as examples for future classes.

CSI Daily Agenda

Plan your own daily agenda. Copy this page for each day of your CSI.

Objectives for Today:

Activities for Today:

CSI in the Classroom

CSI Job Descriptions

Sign-Up Sheet

Directions: Read through all job descriptions. As a team, agree on a job for each team member for the entire **CSI.** Write student's name near the job.

Police Officer(s)

You will interview the victim (complainant) who reports the original crime.

You will photograph, dust for prints, and examine the original crime scene (Crime Scene A).

With information gained, you will write an Investigation Report. This report will contain specific details about the crime scene and the evidence you found, as well as what you chose to do with the evidence.

You will also interview suspects and complete a Suspect Report for each one questioned. Interview questions and answers will be attached to each report.

#1 _____

#2 _____

Detective(s)

You will interview the victim (complainant) who reports the new information about the crime.

You will go to Crime Scene B to photograph, dust for prints, and examine the scene.

You will be responsible for writing an Investigation Report. This report will contain specific details about the crime scene and the evidence you found, as well as what you chose to do with the evidence.

You will also interview suspects and complete a Suspect Report for each one questioned. Interview questions and answers will be attached to each report.

#1 _____

#2 _____

Forensic Scientist(s)

You will perform lab work based on what the police and detectives ask.

You will write a detailed Crime Lab Analysis Report for each activity you do. This will describe the steps you took in analyzing evidence and an explanation of why you performed the lab activity. (For instance, you might state that you were asked by a police officer to analyze something.)

You are also responsible to see that a scale drawing or model of each crime scene is completed.

#1 _____

#2 _____

Police Chief

You are the team leader. It is your responsibility to see that each team member does his or her job well. If your team has questions for your teacher, you are the one that asks. If needed, you will assist the police officers or detectives in investigation of the crime scenes.

You will mostly stay in the office (classroom). You will create two public broadcasts about the CSI.

You will look over all team reports, demanding additional details if needed. And, if you feel a report "won't hold up in court," you will ask for a new one.

You will approve Search Warrant Affidavits if they are well prepared, and deny them if they don't have enough information or probable cause.

You will oversee all reports before they are submitted to the prosecutor (your teacher).

#1 _____

CSI Team Reports

Each team is responsible for the following reports:

Incident Report

The Incident Report is a brief report based on the first call or contact that tells about the crime and thus begins the CSI. This report comes from information given by the victim the first time you hear from her or him. It should include as much detail as is possible to gain before the investigation begins. Try to include the who, what, when, why, where, and how of the crime.

Investigation Report

Information obtained from the victim: The narrative should explain the nature of the incident, tell what was reported, describe what the officer (or detective) was doing at the time the report came in, detail the progression of events until an officer arrived at the crime scene, and include any other relevant facts. The narrative should also give an exact location of the scene where the incident occurred, including street address, city, county, and state.

Date and time: The narrative must describe, as precisely as possible, the day of the week, date, and time the incident occurred. It should also include the date and time the complaint was made.

Scene: Include the time that the officer (or detective) arrived at the scene, the officer's initial observations, and the steps taken to protect the scene. Information from the first person at the scene (other than the officer) should be included.

Stolen property: List and fully describe all stolen property in as much detail as possible. Include such information as size, color, shape, distinguishing characteristics, and money value or sentimental value.

Victim: Give details about the victim: full name, race, gender, date of birth, address, phone number, driver's license number, and social security number. Write a clear physical description of the victim. If money or property is missing from a business or institution, include that name as well.
Note: *Use fabricated addresses, phone numbers, drivers' license numbers, and social security numbers.*

CSI in the Classroom

Evidence: This report should list each piece of evidence seized, its description, location, a photograph, and its measurements (if relevant). Name the investigator who collected it, and include the date and time of its collection. Add a statement describing steps that were taken to preserve all evidence. Much of this information can be transferred from your Evidence List and evidence tags, if you prepared those documents carefully.

Latent prints: Describe all attempts to find and obtain fingerprints, and give details of any results. If fingerprints were lifted from any surfaces, this information should be noted in the report. Make sure this information matches that from your fingerprint evidence tags.

Recovered property: If the case involves any missing property, a detailed report must be written when it is found. Include in this report the name of the person who found it, the location where it was found, and the time and date of its discovery. Also include any other information that is relevant or any evidence that may lead to a conviction or to more suspects. This missing property is also evidence and should be included on your Evidence List, in the Evidence Report, and on an evidence tag.

A separate report is to be filed for each suspect or victim (complainant) questioned.

Title: Title each report "Suspect Report,_____."
person's first and last name

Suspect: Provide the full name, race, gender, date of birth, physical description, address, phone number, driver's license number, and social security number for each suspect. Include any known places of employment, hangouts, habits, or friends of the suspect. Explain why this person is a suspect. Summarize the person's alibi, if there is one. Be sure you have a report for each person listed on your team's Suspect List.

> ***Note***: *Use fabricated addresses, phone numbers, drivers' license numbers, and social security numbers.*

Interviews: Attach to this report a list of all questions asked of this suspect and all the answers given. Include the date, time, and place of the interview. Note names of persons present during the interview.

Crime Lab Analysis Report

A separate report is to be filed for each lab performed.

Reason: Explain who asked you to perform this lab and why.

Details and procedure: Identify the time and date of the lab. Identify the evidence that was examined. Describe the steps that were taken during the lab to analyze the evidence.

Results: Describe the results and any conclusions drawn from them.

Scale Drawings or Model
This is a visual report.

Scale drawings: Use graph paper to draw both crime scenes. Side A of the graph paper is the original crime scene. Side B of the paper is the second crime scene. Everything should be labeled and drawn to scale. Make a key for each drawing.

Models: If a model is made for a crime scene, make sure that it is titled, labeled, and has a key.

Crime Scene Photographs

Mount and prepare all photographs taken at the crime scenes. Label these A and B, to match the crime scenes. Describe each photograph with a detailed caption.

Police Chief Public News Broadcasts

Two public news briefings are to be prepared by the team's police chief. These reports will be written and may be filmed if a video camera is available. Prepare the reports according to the instructions on the Police Chief Public News Broadcast form provided to your team.

Final Report

This report includes information and details from all of the above reports. It should fully state, beyond a reasonable doubt, the solution to the crime. And it must explain what details and clues helped you solve the crime. Follow the Final Report Outline provided to your team.

Final Report Outline

Use this as an outline for your formal written report. Include all details. Edit and revise more than once and by more than one person. This group effort will receive a group grade.

I. The Crime (introductory paragraph)

A. The incident

B. Progression of events

C. Location where incident occurred (exact place)

D. Time incident occurred (as close as possible)

II. The Crime Scene

A. Steps taken to protect the scene

B. Victim

    1. Name and address (school)

    2. Physical description

C. Photographer of crime scene

    1. Name, job position

    2. Kind of camera

D. Evidence

    1. List of evidence found

    2. Time and location found

    3. Description of each piece of evidence

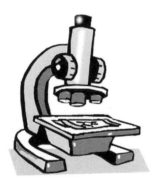

III. Latent Prints

A. Successful attempts to obtain prints

    1. Location, object

    2. Match with fingerprint templates

B. Unsuccessful attempts

    1. Location, object

    2. Why results were inconclusive

IV. Stolen Property

A. List of stolen property

B. Detailed description of each item

C. Value of each item

V. Victim Interviews

A. Time, date, location for each

B. Questions and answers

　　1. Recounting of questions

　　2. Recounting of victim answers

C. Summary of victim statement

VI. Suspects

A. Name, address (school) of each

B. Detailed description of each

C. Place of employment, job of each

D. Evidence leading to suspicion of guilt for each

VII. Solution (concluding paragraph)

A. Conclusion as to who is guilty

B. Reasons for your team's conclusion

　　1. Evidence to support

　　2. Probable cause

　　3. Investigation details

REMINDERS

This is a competition. Do not discuss your results, thoughts, or ideas with any members of another team.

Assessment is based on your conclusion and overall quality of the work you submit.

You will also do an evaluation of the team members, where you will offer some thoughts on the participation of your peers and yourself.

CSI in the Classroom

scoring
CSI
rubric

CSI Scoring Rubric

Since the work of the crime-scene investigation falls to the CSI teams, the CSI Scoring Rubric is designed as a tool to assess the process and accomplishments of the team. It is critical for students to identify the goals for a learning project. The scoring rubric, in combination with the description of required team reports (pages 65–69), shows students where they are headed, what to do, how to do it well, and how to tell when they meet the goal.

The CSI Scoring Rubric on page 72 is directly correlated to the list of CSI team reports on pages 65–67. The instructions that accompany the scoring rubric direct students to keep the list of reports beside the rubric as they work. The list gives definite criteria for preparing reports. The rubric shows the point value of each of those reports and the components of the reports. Together, the rubric and report list provide a solid base for helping students succeed.

Directions:

1. Make copies of the CSI Scoring Rubric Team Information sheet along with the CSI Scoring Rubric (pages 71 and 72).

2. Distribute the rubric and information sheet to each team.

3. Review the scoring process with students. Remind students to keep these criteria in mind as they work through the CSI.

4. Remind students to keep rubrics and information sheets in the team folders.

Note: This rubric can serve as a guide, but it might not be exactly what you wish to use for evaluation. The point values may not suit your purposes. Change, rearrange, reassign points, and adapt the rubric as fits your own CSI plans.

CSI Scoring Rubric

Team Information

What is the CSI Scoring Rubric?	

- The CSI Scoring Rubric assigns a score value (number of points) to each of your required team reports for the CSI.

- It sets out a plan for your team to earn 200 points by doing your work well.

How does it work?

- The rubric is directly connected to your list of CSI Team Reports, which is in your team folder.

- The list of CSI Team Reports shows you what reports need to be written and submitted. This list, along with the outline for the final report, also describes what should be IN each report. So if you follow these, you will know how to do each report well.

- The rubric shows the total point values for each report and a breakdown of points for specific parts of some reports.

How does it help us do our CSI team work?

- The rubric, along with the list of reports and the final report outline, shows you exactly what you need to do to succeed as a team.

- The list of reports sets the goals for a good performance.

- The rubric shows you just how to reach the goals.

What should we do with it?

- Lay the rubric beside the report list.

- Keep paying attention to the description of each report as you prepare it.

- If you follow the guidelines for your reports, you'll be able to start piling up the points!

CSI in the Classroom

CSI
Scoring
Rubric

Team_____

Final Team Score*_____ points of 200 total points

Report, Requirements		Score of Possible Score
Incident Report**		_____ of 10
Investigation Reports**		
Information obtained from victim	_____ of 10 possible points	
Date and time of incident and complaint	_____ of 10 possible points	_____ of 50
Scene, arrival, steps taken, information	_____ of 10 possible points	
Stolen property	_____ of 10 possible points	
Victim	_____ of 10 possible points	
Evidence Report		
Evidence seized, description, preservation	_____ of 5 possible points	_____ of 10
Latent prints, attempts to find, results	_____ of 5 possible points	
Recovered Property Report		_____ of 10
Suspect Reports**		
Suspect description, and reason for suspicion	_____ of 10 possible points	
Interview questions asked of suspect	_____ of 10 possible points	_____ of 30
Interview answers given by suspect	_____ of 10 possible points	
Crime Lab Analysis Reports**		
Reason (who asked for the lab and why)	_____ of 5 possible points	
Time and date of lab	_____ of 5 possible points	_____ of 30
Details and procedure	_____ of 10 possible points	
Results	_____ of 10 possible points	
Crime Scene Photographs**		
Correct labels	_____ of 10 possible points	_____ of 10
Adequate captions	_____ of 10 possible points	
Scale Drawings & Models		
Accurate representation of Crime Scene A	_____ of 5 possible points	_____ of 10
Accurate representation of Crime Scene B	_____ of 5 possible points	
Police Chief Public News Broadcasts**		_____ of 10
Final Report		_____ of 20
Accuracy, neatness of all reports		_____ of 5
Appropriate titles on all reports		_____ of 5

*Use the CSI Team Reports list and Final Report Outline for details of each report.
** For multiple reports in a category, points will be split among the reports.

CSI Terminlogy

The terminology worksheet is a beginning activity designed to help students become familiar with the language of forensics and investigations right from the start. If students forget the meaning of certain terms, they can use this sheet as a reference throughout the CSI. Team members should work together to find the definitions. Then students can work on the drawings while other teammates are out investigating a crime scene.

> Did the latent prints provide evidence of a larceny?

Directions:

1. Supply dictionaries or appropriate Internet sites for students to explore definitions of words useful in forensic activities.

2. Be sure that each team has a copy of the CSI Terminology Worksheet.

3. The directions are printed at the top of the first sheet. Review these with students so they understand what is required. Encourage them to "think outside the box" when deciding on what to draw. They do not have to actually draw the literal meaning of the word. Suggest that they brainstorm ideas for each drawing.

4. Once students have completed the worksheet, reinforce understanding of the words frequently. Use these words repeatedly as you discuss CSI proceedings. Ask students to define, compare, demonstrate, give examples, and otherwise elaborate on these words to show that they fully understand the meanings.

> Chromatography and graphology led us to Max as the writer of the note. But he has a tight alibi.

> A witness saw Mr. Hall put a large package in a van at the crime scene. This gave probable cause to search the van.

DO NOT CROSS LINE CRIME

CSI Terminology Worksheet

Directions: Use a dictionary or Internet sites to find definitions for the following terms. Draw or find a picture or symbol to show that you understand the meaning of each word.

1. larceny

2. forensic science

3. evidence

4. artifact

5. latent fingerprints

6. inked prints

7. chromatography

_____
_____
_____
_____
_____

8. scale drawing

_____
_____
_____
_____
_____

9. probable cause

_____
_____
_____
_____
_____

10. search warrant affidavit

_____
_____
_____
_____
_____

11. complainant

_____
_____
_____
_____
_____

12. graphology

_____
_____
_____
_____
_____

13. alibi

_____
_____
_____
_____
_____

DO NOT CROSS LINE CRI

75

CSI Activity Log

Record your daily activities in the space provided. Give specific details.

DO NOT CROSS CRIME SCENE DO NO

DATE	CSI ACTIVITIES I DID TODAY

Name _____   CSI Team _____

CSI Mounting Photos

If you have a camera for students to use, you will want to add this activity to your CSI investigation. Use of a digital camera will also require availability of a printer to print the photos. If a digital camera is not available to students, use another type of camera and arrange for quick development of the photos. Or take pictures of the scenes when you set them up, develop the pictures, and give two photos of each crime scene to each team.

Explanation to give to students:

This assignment uses photos that the police officers and detectives take while investigating Crime Scene A and Crime Scene B. These photos are to be carefully displayed in preparation for presentation in a courtroom. Students will mount two photos from each of the crime scenes, clearly labeling and describing the photos.

- Crime Scene A is the location of the theft or other incident.
- Crime Scene B is the location where the stolen object is recovered or some other new evidence is discovered.

Directions:

1. Provide students with card stock or poster board and glue for mounting photos.

2. Emphasize that the photos of a crime scene are critical to the "evidence trail." These photos must be carefully and professionally mounted, labeled, and explained.

3. Students will neatly mount two photos of Crime Scene A to one side of the paper and two photos of Crime Scene B to the other side.

4. Instruct teams to include a label and date on each side, and a detailed caption beneath each photo.

CSI Mounting Photos

Team Information

Prepare your photographs of the crime scenes carefully to be presented as evidence in a courtroom.

1. Begin with a piece of card stock, poster board, or construction paper.

2. Label one side A for photos from Crime Scene A. Add the date. Label the other side B for photos of Crime Scene B. Add the date.

3. Glue two photos of Crime Scene A on one side. Add a caption for each photo that describes it in detail.

4. Glue two photos of Crime Scene B on the other side. Add a caption for each photo that describes it in detail.

CSI Scale Drawings

This activity is a great addition to any CSI investigation. Your artistic students will enjoy assisting in the drawing of each crime scene. This makes use of math skills, map skills, and organizational skills, as well. The scale drawing should be done on graph paper.

Explanation to give to students:

1. The scale drawing represents the physical layout of a crime scene in a small version, drawn to a mathematical scale. It must cover the entire width and length of the crime-scene area. All furniture and objects present at the scene must be drawn in the correct location, just as found by the investigators. The measurements of the crime scene are crucial in creating an accurate scale drawing.

2. Each team is to present a drawing of each crime scene. Crime Scene A is the location of the theft or other incident. Crime Scene B is the location where the stolen object is recovered or some other new evidence is discovered.

3. The drawing should be neat and well presented to be used as evidence in a courtroom. All items should be labeled. A scale and a key must be included.

Directions:

1. Supply two pieces of graph paper or plain white paper for each team.

2. Share the above explanation with students.

3. Review the concept of scale drawing with students. Discuss how to choose a scale and use it for the drawing. If needed, practice some simple scale drawings. For instance, students can create a scale drawing of the top of the teacher's desk.

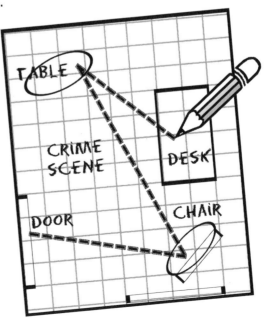

Alternative to scale drawings:

Encourage teams who wish to explore other artistic representations to try three-dimensional models of one crime scene or both crime scenes. A well-presented, well-labeled model to scale can replace the scale drawing.

79

CSI
Suspect List

Directions:
Tell why each is a suspect. Record the alibi.
Remember to verify each alibi.

Victim/Suspect	Why?	Alibi
A	a	a
B	b	b
C	c	c
D	d	d
E	e	e
F	f	f
G	g	g

CSI Search Warrants

A **search warrant** is a document giving a law enforcement officer legal permission to search a dwelling or place of business, or to obtain various kinds of samples that may be evidence in a crime. A warrant can only be obtained after an affidavit is presented, requesting such permission. The **affidavit** is a written document giving a defensible reason (probable cause) for obtaining certain kinds of information from a suspect or victim. This includes such things as teeth bite mark impressions, writing samples, hair or fiber samples, fingerprints, body fluids (saliva, blood), surveillances, phone or credit card records, DNA samples, or personal belongings. A warrant is also needed if an officer intends to search someone's dwelling or car.

Explanation to give to students:

1. When you want to obtain something from a victim or suspect, you must complete a Search Warrant Affidavit and submit it to your team's police chief for review. Then submit it to the prosecuting attorney (your teacher) and judge (if there is someone acting in that role) for approval. The affidavit must include probable cause for obtaining the items. If yours does not, it will be denied. You will have to rewrite it or continue to investigate other avenues.

2. If your affidavit is approved, you will be given an Approved Search Warrant form. You must show this to each person from whom you are taking samples. After you execute the search warrant, you must create a written account of the items seized and actions taken. Write this on a new sheet of paper and staple it to the original Search Warrant Affidavit. (This is a short report. For example: *One bicycle retrieved with make, model, and serial number.* That is it!)

Directions:

1. Make several copies of the Search Warrant Affidavit (page 82). Put these in a place where students can access them easily.

2. Make several copies of the Approved Search Warrant (page 83). Keep these in your possession. Complete one for each affidavit that you approve. Staple a copy of this to the original affidavit requesting the warrant. Be sure to sign and date all approved search warrants.

3. Remind students that the teacher has all records of fingerprints for victims and suspects. Teams must present a completed affidavit to the teacher before borrowing any fingerprint templates.

CSI in the Classroom

CSI SEARCH WARRANT AFFIDAVIT

State of _____

_____
(Judicial District)

Team _____

Date _____

Case # _____

1. The person, place, or thing to be searched is described as:

   and is located at:

2. The PROPERTY to be searched for, and seized if found, is
   specifically described as:

3. The FACTS establishing probable cause or the grounds for
   search are:

   This affidavit consists of _____ pages.

   _____
   Affiant (Officer or Detective)

Reviewed on	Reviewed on	Suscribed and sworn to before me on
_____ date	_____ date	_____ date
By	By	By
_____ Team's Police Chief	_____ Prosecuting Attorney	_____ Judge/Magistrate

CSI APPROVED SEARCH WARRANT

IN THE NAME OF THE PEOPLE OF THE STATE OF _____:

I have found that probable cause exists and you are commanded to make the search and seize the described property. Show this Warrant (with Search Warrant Affidavit attached) to the person from whom you need to obtain personal property, handwriting samples, fingerprints, or other items. You are further commanded to promptly return this warrant and a detailed written tabulation below to the court (your teacher).

Issued: _____ _____
Today's Date Prosecuting Attorney (Teacher)

Tabulation (Written Inventory Report)

Search was made on _____ and the following property was seized by _____:
Date Prosecuting Attorney (Teacher)

Completed warrant with tabulation turned in on

Date _____ _____
Prosecuting Attorney (Teacher)

From _____ _____
Officer/Detective Team name

83

CSI Evidence List

Directions:

1. Use this list to record all items present at Crime Scene A and Crime Scene B that you feel are relevant to solving the case.

2. When you return from your investigation, present this list to your teacher to retrieve evidence tags for the items you listed.

3. If you'd like to analyze or compare fingerprints, teeth impressions, ink pigments, or other samples from any suspect or victim, you must first write a Search Warrant Affidavit that includes probable cause. Write a separate affidavit for each suspect. Submit it to your police chief for review. He or she will pass it on to the prosecuting attorney (teacher).

4. If you are granted an Approved Search Warrant, you must present it to the prosecuting attorney to compare it with your evidence tags.

Crime Scene A Evidence List

Crime Scene B Evidence List

SCENE DO NOT CROSS CRIME SCENE DO NOT CR

CSI in the Classroom

Copyright ©2009 by Incentive Publications, Inc., Nashville, TN.

CSI Evidence Tags for Fingerprints

Explanation to give to students:

- The team police officers and detectives on CSI teams will need to use evidence tags when they find fingerprints at a crime scene. When a print is lifted, place the tape with the print directly onto the evidence tag in the rectangular space.

- The police officer or detective who obtained the print should fill in the rest of the information on the tag.

- The print is later examined by the team's forensic scientist(s) who will use the Fingerprint Classification Sheet (page 104) to determine the type of print. It will also be compared to the Suspect Fingerprint Templates to look for a match to a suspect.

- The tags are to be kept in team folders and used throughout the case.

Directions:

1. Make several copies of the Evidence Tags for Fingerprints templates (page 86) and store them in a place where students can obtain them easily. Or give a few to each team to keep in the team folder.

2. Explain how these tags are to be used when investigators find fingerprints at the crime scene.

Sample:

Evidence Tag for Fingerprints

Print Taken From ___*Cola can*___

Obtained by ___*Detective Bobby Jones*___

Team ___*Third Street Five*___ Date ___*3-13-2009*___

Location (Crime Scene) ___*west office at G.M.S*___

Forensic Scientist ___*Sally Peters*___

What type of print is this? *plain whorl*

CSI in the Classroom

CSI Evidence Tag for Fingerprints

(Template)

Evidence Tag for Fingerprints

Print Taken From _____

Obtained By _____

Team _____ Date _____

Location (Crime Scene): _____

Forensic Scientist _____

What type of print is this?

Evidence Tag for Fingerprints

Print Taken From _____

Obtained By _____

Team _____ Date _____

Location (Crime Scene) _____

Forensic Scientist _____

What type of print is this?

Evidence Tag for Fingerprints

Print Taken From _____

Obtained By _____

Team _____ Date _____

Location (Crime Scene) _____

Forensic Scientist _____

What type of print is this?

CSI Evidence Tags for Artifacts

CSI evidence tags

Explanation to give to students:

- When an item of interest is found at a crime scene, do not touch it. Take photos of the item and record the information about the item on an evidence tag.

- The team police officers and detectives should complete an evidence tag for each item that is noticed at the crime scene that they believe is relevant to the crime. All tags are to be brought back to the classroom.

- After all teams have finished combing the crime scene, the evidence or artifacts of interest can be further investigated or brought into the classroom.

- All evidence tags are to be kept in team folders and used throughout the case.

Directions:

1. Make several copies of the Evidence Tags for Artifacts template (page 88) and store them in a place where students can obtain them easily. Or give several to each team to keep in the team folder.

2. Explain how these tags are to be used when investigators find artifacts at the crime scene.

Sample:

Evidence Tag for Artifact

Date Retrieved _*March 13*_ Time _*10:15 am*_

Location Where Evidence Was Found _*empty office in Counseling Office*_

Item _*half-eaten candy bar*_ Officer _*Jennifer Martin*_

Taken From _*table in center of office*_

Comments _*note teeth marks*_

Team _*5th Period Experts*_

CSI Evidence Tag for Artifacts
(Template)

Evidence Tag for Artifact

Date Retrieved _____Time_____

Location Where Evidence Was Found_____

Item_____Officer_____

Taken From_____

Comments_____

Team_____

Evidence Tag for Artifact

Date Retrieved _____Time_____

Location Where Evidence Was Found_____

Item_____Officer_____

Taken From_____

Comments_____

Team_____

CSI Police Chief Public News Broadcast

When a crime-scene investigation is newsworthy, a TV or radio program may be interrupted by a short news broadcast. The officer in charge of the investigation holds a conference to brief the news media and the public about the progress of the investigation. This is an excellent opportunity for the police chief from each team to use his or her public-speaking skills in front of a video camera. Share the directions below with each team, so that they understand what must be included in each broadcast.

Each news broadcast taping should be done in privacy, as the suspects, evidence, and analysis are confidential for each team. Enlist the help of a trusted volunteer to supervise tapings in a quiet area outside of the classroom.

The first news broadcast:

After the first investigation of Crime Scene A and interview of the victim, students begin the Incident Report. The police chief from each team should take enough information from that report to create a news broadcast of about two or three minutes in length. This report is to be prepared on the Police Chief Public News Broadcast form (page 90). When it is ready, the news brief can be presented before the video camera. The forensic scientist on each team can help by working the video camera. The report should be presented on the fourth or fifth day of the CSI.

Discuss with students the idea that answering all the questions at this early point in the investigation is impossible. However, the news brief should include as much detail as possible (based on the information collected so far). It is important to refrain from giving away too much information to the public about whom the team believes may or may not be guilty.

The second news broadcast:

After each team has fully investigated and come to a conclusion about what happened (and about the guilty parties), the police chief on each team should write a second news broadcast (using the same form as above). This report includes the who, what, when, why, where, and how of the crime. A fictional or actual apprehension of the guilty suspect should be included, as should a public acknowledgement of the chief's CSI team and their efforts. This broadcast is to be five to eight minutes in length.

Police Chief Public News Broadcast

Directions to the police chief:

1. The first broadcast gives a brief summary of information known about the crime so far. It is two to three minutes long. Include only the details appropriate to share with the public at this time.

2. The second broadcast is five to eight minutes long, and includes the who, what, when, why, where and how of the crime. It also includes a report of the apprehension of a suspect who is presumed guilty.

3. Before you videotape this, the report must have your signature and your teacher's approval. Keep this written script in the team folder.

4. Check the appropriate box:

First Broadcast ☐   Second Broadcast ☐

_____

_____

_____

_____

_____

_____

_____

_____

_____

_____

_____

_____

_____

_____   _____
Police Chief Signature   Teacher Approval (initials)

Chromatography During the  CSI

If you decide to incorporate any kind of note or written item that is left at a crime scene, students will need the following page to assist them with the chromatography investigation. You can keep all of the suspects' pens of different types, just as you might keep the suspects' fingerprint templates or bite impression templates. Or, you can give each suspect a specific pen and ask that they keep that pen aside until a student approaches them for it with a search warrant. In either case, make sure each pen is clearly labeled with the name of the suspect.

Note: If your CSI involves a note or anything that includes a written sample, students will have the opportunity to analyze both the chromatography and the handwriting. Be sure that students have participated in the chromatography and handwriting prelabs, and that they have the sheets from those labs available as they investigate the note during the CSI.

Directions:

1. Arrange for the guilty suspect to write several copies of the note on chromatography paper (coffee filter paper) with a specific pen.

2. Place one of these copies at the crime scene.

3. After all teams have investigated the crime scene, look at the evidence list and tags to see which teams listed a note as evidence. If this is on the team's list, give the team one of the copies of the note. (Or, if you just have one copy, cut the note into pieces, so each team can analyze the pen used.)

4. Provide each team a copy of the CSI Ink Analysis Worksheet on page 92. Review the directions and procedure with students.

5. Remind students that they must write a Search Warrant Affidavit if they intend to request a pen from a suspect. Remind them also, that they must present the suspect with an Approved Search Warrant.

CSI Ink Analysis Team Worksheet

Directions:

1. Prepare a strip of chromatography paper (coffee filter) for each suspect whose pen you wish to analyze. Write the suspect's name in the top section of the strip, leaving at least two inches blank at the bottom of the strip. Present an Approved Search Warrant for each ink sample you request. Use the suspect's pen to draw a line about an inch from the bottom of the strip.

2. Bring the sample back to the classroom forensic lab. Follow the procedures that you learned in the chromatography prelab to analyze each sample.

3. Perform the same procedures on the evidence sample of the note from the crime scene.

Glue a small sample of the evidence note here.

SOLVENT	Suspect A	Suspect B	Suspect C	Suspect D	Suspect E	Suspect F
WATER						
Dry the paper strips. Glue a small sample in the box.						

4. Compare your results. According to your analysis, which of the suspects' pens match the sample found at the crime scene?

Explain your answer:

Reminder: Write a descriptive report explaining the results of each analysis. Attach this to the appropriate Search Warrant Affidavit.

Name_____Date_____

Your CSI Ends

CRIME SCENE DO NOT CROSS CRIME SCENE DO NOT C

CRIME SCENE DO NOT CROSS CRIME SCENE DO NOT

Celebrating Your CSI

CSI Team Review

CSI Reflection

Beyond the CSI

Celebrating Your CSI

Plan a final event to share and celebrate all the serious detecting, clever thinking, discoveries, surprises, and teamwork of your crime scene investigation. Invite everyone who participated in the CSI, as well as parents and friends.

CSI PARTY MENU

ALIBI BITES APPETIZERS

POLICE BADGE CUT-OUT SANDWICHES

THUMBPRINT COOKIES

MYSTERY CUPCAKES

SECRET-RECIPE PUNCH

Follow the yellow footprints to the

CSI CELEBRATION

Friday, Sept. 19 at 3:10 PM

School Library

See and hear the results of our
2008 Crime Scene Investigations.
Enjoy CSI music,
CSI snacks, and
CSI adventures.

*Bring a magnifying glass
and a flashlight.*

Relax! You are not under suspicion!
Security provided by CSI teams
from Mrs. Kennedy's English class

Add some of these to your celebration:

Design and create fun, fetching invitations for guests.

Make party favors in "evidence bags" with "evidence tags."

Create some original music.
Write CSI words set to familiar tunes.
Make up and perform a rap about your CSI.

Choose favorite music (including some mysterious-sounding tunes) and make up original dances (such as the Sleuth Shuffle, the Detective's Groove, the Forensic Funk, or a Hip-Hop Through the Crime Scene).

Decorate with fingerprint art, crime scene tape, footprints, badges, magnifying glasses, mystery notes, and other CSI supplies.

Greet the visitors with clues they can follow to play some game or search for goodies and prizes.

Introduce and honor the suspects, victims, and volunteers.

Show off the results of your CSI.
Share some of the evidence. Let teams take turns explaining how they arrived at conclusions they reached.

Tell why some of the suspects were exonerated.

If you filmed any of the CSI activities, include a picture show or display.

Give tours through the CSI forensic lab.

Give away class-made badges or T-shirts and other inexpensive (or free) prizes.

CSI Team Review

Think about how your team worked during the CSI experience. Evaluate the contribution of each team member to the CSI.

- List each team member. Include yourself! Carefully read the descriptions within each category and the explanations of the scores.
- Assign a score of 1, 2, 3, 4, or 5 to each person in each category.

5 = **Excellent Team Member**—did these things consistently and very well

4 = **Strong Team Member**—mostly fit these descriptions most of the time

3 = **Adequate Team Member**—sometimes fit these descriptions

2 = **Somewhat Unreliable Team Member**—took part, but couldn't be counted on

1 = **Unreliable Team Member**—fulfilled very few, if any, of the requirements

Your Name_____ Team_____

	Self						
Team member name or initials							
Team Job **P** = police officer **D** = detective **S** = scientist **C** = police chief							
Participation - took part in all CSI activities eagerly - was ready to work and discuss - contributed to group decisions and reports - followed all procedures well							
Job Performance - stayed within his or her job description - let others do their jobs - did all reports required of his or her particular job							
Cooperation - worked well with other team members - seemed anxious for the team to succeed - had a positive attitude toward the CSI and the team - kept team business **CONFIDENTIAL**							

CSI in the Classroom

CSI Reflection

Your name_____

Take some time to reflect on what happened for you during CSI preparations and activities. Complete the sentences.

My most important contribution to the CSI process was

An important thing I learned from the CSI unit was

What I liked most about the CSI was

If I could do a different job on the CSI team next time, it would be _____ because

A skill that I improved as a result of the CSI was

The hardest part for me was

The most helpful prelab for me was

What surprised me most about the CSI experience was

Something I learned during the CSI that connects to my real life outside school was

In general, I feel _____ about my part in the CSI because

Something that could be added or changed when planning the next CSI is

Use the back of this page for anything else you would like to say about the CSI or how you felt about your part in the CSI.

CSI in the Classroom   96

Beyond the CSI

beyond the
CSI

Don't let the excitement, growth, and cooperative spirit of the CSI end when the unit is over. Keep the good outcomes alive and expand them to enrich learning throughout the rest of the school year.

Give students a chance to debrief.

You may be ready to go on to another unit and another topic, but students need time to process the CSI experience. Plan some sessions for them to discuss what they experienced, to identify skills they learned or strengthened, and to make connections with other subjects and other situations in their lives.

Continue and deepen the CSI skills.

Plan situations in which students are required to:
- observe, question, interview, gather information
- outline, summarize, paraphrase, and record
- analyze and evaluate
- plan and organize
- draw conclusions and reach solutions
- communicate conclusions (orally and in writing)
- explain, argue, and defend judgments or solutions
- reflect on their performance in any academic setting

Continue the emphasis on "following the evidence."

One of the most important processes in the CSI experience—carefully gathering evidence and using it to arrive at solutions or substantiate conclusions—has widespread application to every subject area and many situations outside school. Make use of this experience. Keep students focused on this habit of supporting conclusions with evidence.

Continue the teamwork.

Capitalize on the cooperative spirit and the benefits of cooperation. Plan frequent classroom activities that involve group collaboration. Those are critical skills to keep alive!

Continue the cross-curricular emphasis.

The CSI unit (depending on how your planned it) combines language, science, social skills, math, and possibly other disciplines. Keep planning learning events that mix disciplines.

CSI in the Classroom

Extend the CSI investigative mindset.

Take advantage of the CSI spirit of curiosity to keep using critical thinking skills in any subject area. Ask questions such as these to stimulate reasoning and incite good discussions. Train students to ask these kinds of questions.

Why did this happen?

What difference does this make?

What's new about this information?

What can be inferred from this?

What other situations does this affect?

What other questions would you ask?

Where does this lead?

How does this relate to you?

Why is this important?

Is this reasoning sound?

Are the ideas stated clearly?

What does this mean?

Is the evidence credible?

How effective is this?

How might someone else see this differently?

What are the possible outcomes of this?

What factors influenced this viewpoint?

What evidence supports this conclusion?

How does this viewpoint compare to someone else's?

What is the writer's (speaker's) purpose?

What is the underlying belief, theme, or message?

What makes this effective (or ineffective)?

What are the implications of _____ ?

What is the effect of _____ on _____ ?

What information is relevant (or not relevant) to our purpose?

How does _____ relate to _____ ?

If this evidence is introduced, how is our solution affected?

What judgment would you make about this observation?

What causes are obvious (or not obvious)?

How has this information changed my judgment?

What makes this situation unique?

Of this statement, what is impartial observation and what is judgment?

How does your experience affect your view of _____ ?

What does someone need to know in order to solve this problem?

If _____ is true, how does _____ change?

What are the consequences of this choice? What are the benefits?

CSI Prelabs

Master List of Supplies
Observations & Inferences Lab
Fingerprint Lab
Bite Impressions Lab
Handwriting Lab
Mystery Substances Lab
Chromatography Lab
Textiles Lab

CRIME SCENE DO NOT CROSS CRIME SCENE DO NOT

CSI Prelab Supplies

Master List

Observations & Inferences Lab
notebooks
pencils or pens
Observations & Inferences Lab Sheets

Fingerprint Lab (I and II)
number 2 pencils
paper
clear cellophane tape
assorted inked fingerprint samples
soda cans or clear drinking glasses
magnifying glasses
latex gloves
fingerprint dusting powder
  and brushes (optional)
Fingerprint Lab Sheets I and II
Fingerprint Lab Permission Slips
Fingerprint Classification Guides

Handwriting Lab (I and II)
half-sheets of paper
pencils
magnifying glasses
handwriting samples
Handwriting Lab Sheets I and II

Chromatography Lab
pencils
coffee filters cut into strips
250 mL beakers
cellophane tape and glue
scissors
water
mystery note on a coffee filter
six different pens labeled A–F
Chromatography Lab Sheets

Bite Impressions Lab
Styrofoam cups
pens or pencils
glue or tape
apples
cubes of cheese
Bite Impressions Lab Sheets

Mystery Substances Lab
cafeteria trays
glue stick
clear contact paper
plastic wrap
Popsicle sticks
magnifying glasses
microscopes (optional)
eyedroppers
paper plates
measuring spoons
baking powder
baking soda
cornstarch
sugar
vinegar
water
iodine solution
Mystery Substances Lab Sheets
Powder Analysis Charts

Textiles Lab
microscopes, slides,
  slide covers
scraps of textiles:
  nylon, cotton,
  silk, wool
Textile Lab Sheets

CSI in the Classroom

CSI Observations & Inferences Lab

Goals of this lab:

- to address misconceptions that arise from individual observations
- to enhance skills of observation and inference needed
  to carry out investigations and experiments

Explanation:

People may report observations with certainty. However, their observations do differ, depending on factors such as location, what they pay attention to, their personal biases, their past experiences, and their prior knowledge. In this lab, students will view an incident that occurs without warning. Then they will answer some questions about what they observed. When their observations and inferences are shared, they will notice how other people have different interpretations of the same event.

Materials needed:

- notebook or paper, pencil or pen
- copies of Observations & Inferences Lab Sheet

Directions:

1. Find a co-worker to stage a confrontation, coming into your classroom and accusing you of something. If possible, choose someone the students do not know well. (It is helpful to have a script so you know the general direction of the conversation and have accurate quotes for later discussions.) When the time is right in the schedule, stage the incident.

2. Pass out copies of the Observations & Inferences Lab Sheet. Discuss and complete the definitions together. Once students understand the terms, they can complete the first ten questions.

3. Discuss and compare their answers to questions 1 through 10.

4. Give them a little more time to complete questions 11 and 12. Then discuss these ideas:
   a) In order to have correct inferences, your observations must be accurate and not biased.
   b) You can change results or an outcome of a situation if your initial observations are biased about what is going on.

5. Repeat this lab by staging other events that students observe (without prior warning or preparation).

CSI in the Classroom

CSI Observations & Inferences Lab Sheet

Define observation:

Define inference:

You just witnessed a confrontation! It is your job now to recall observations from this incident and answer the following questions. You will not be penalized for incorrect answers. Answer every question to the best of your ability.

Observations:

1. What color was the visitor's hair?   2. What was the name?

3. What was the visitor wearing?

4. What did the visitor say?

5. What did your teacher say?

6. What hand movements or expressions did you see?

7. What else did you notice about the confrontation?

Inferences:

8. How does the visitor feel about your teacher?

9. How does your teacher feel about the visitor?

10. Did your teacher do what the visitor claimed?

Other Questions:

11. Why is it important to make accurate observations?

12. What can happen if you make inferences based on inaccurate observations?

CSI Fingerprint Lab, Part I

Goals of this lab:

- to learn to take fingerprints
- to use a Fingerprint Classification Guide to analyze and classify fingerprints

Explanation:

This lab gives students the opportunity to make a set of their own inked prints, and then to examine, analyze, and classify them. Because of the personal nature of fingerprints, it is important to have permission from a parent or guardian of each student before doing this lab.

Materials needed:

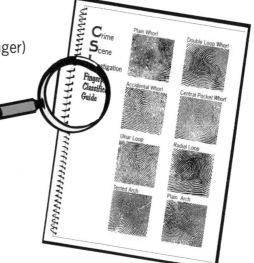

- clear cellophane tape (small piece for each finger)
- number 2 pencils
- magnifying glasses
- extra paper and tape for practice
- assorted inked fingerprint samples
- copies of Fingerprint Lab Sheet for Part I
- Fingerprint Classification Guide
- Fingerprint Permission Slip

Directions:

1. Send copies of the Fingerprint Permission Slip home with students two weeks before the scheduled lab.

2. Pass out copies of the Fingerprint Lab Part I Lab Sheet and guide students through the fingerprinting process.

3. Pass out copies of the Fingerprint Classification Guide along with magnifying glasses. Guide students as they analyze, compare, and classify fingerprints.

4. Give them some anonymous fingerprints that you have collected (individual prints). Let them analyze and classify these also.

CSI in the Classroom

CSI Fingerprint Permission Slip

Dear Parents and/or Guardians:

We are studying different types of fingerprints in the classroom in preparation for an upcoming Crime Scene Investigation, CSI. Students will obtain their own fingerprints and attempt to classify them using a Fingerprint Classification Sheet.

In order to participate in this lab, students must have a permission slip signed by a parent or guardian. If you do not want your child to participate, he or she will be responsible for an independent study assignment.

Thank you for your continuous support. If you have comments, concerns, or suggestions, please feel free to contact me.

Educationally,

- -

Please cut along line, complete, and return.

I, _____, give my child permission to participate in this lab. I understand that this is a learning opportunity only and that the fingerprint record will be destroyed or sent home after the lab is complete.

Student Name_____

Parent/Guardian Signature_____Date_____

* Please return to your teacher by _____Thank You!

CSI Fingerprint Lab Sheet, Part I

rub pencil here

Directions:

1. Rub a number 2 pencil in the box at the top of this sheet until there is a dark smudge of graphite.

2. Beginning with your little finger, rub the entire base of your finger on the smudge until it is covered well with graphite.

3. Place a small piece of tape over your fingertip and press gently.

4. Remove the tape and stick it in the appropriate box on this lab sheet.

5. Repeat this process for all of your fingers and thumbs.

6. Use the Fingerprint Classification Guide to identify the type for each print.

7. Compare your results with your lab partner or another student.

Left Hand

Identify the type of each fingerprint.

Thumb	Index Finger	Middle Finger	Ring Finger	Little Finger

Type:_____ _____ _____ _____ _____

Right Hand Identify the type of each fingerprint.

Thumb	Index Finger	Middle Finger	Ring Finger	Little Finger

Type:_____ _____ _____ _____ _____

Name_____Date_____

CSI in the Classroom

Crime Scene Investigation

Fingerprint Classification Guide

Plain Whorl

Double Loop Whorl

Accidental Whorl

Central Pocket Whorl

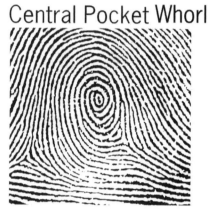

Ulnar Loop

Radial Loop

Tented Arch

Plain Arch

CSI Fingerprint Lab, Part II

Goal of this lab:

To learn to lift latent prints from a surface and preserve the prints

Explanation:

This lab gives students a chance to find latent prints and preserve them. Students can try to identify the owner of the prints by comparing them to the fingerprints of classmates.

Materials needed:

- cellophane tape
- number 2 pencils
- latex gloves
- Fingerprint Classification Guides
- several clean, clear, smooth glasses
- magnifying glasses
- copies of Fingerprint Lab, Part II Sheet
- completed Fingerprint Lab, Part I Sheets

Directions to the teacher:

1. Wearing gloves, clean several glasses well, so they have no fingerprints. (You could use soda pop cans instead of glasses.)

2. Find a way to get fingerprints of one student on each of the glasses. If possible, have all students handle the glasses (some before you clean them well) so they do not know whose prints are on them. Get good prints by greasing the fingers so they leave a print that can be seen well.

3. Make sure students have copies of the Fingerprint Lab Sheet, Part II, as well as their own Fingerprint Templates and Fingerprint Classification Guides.

4. Divide students into groups. Read through all instructions with students. Then give a glass or two to each group. Make sure the glasses have prints from students in that group.

5. After the prints are identified, discuss the process by asking questions such as: How did this work? Was it easy or hard? What problems did you encounter? How could we do it better another time?

An alternative for this lab:

If at all possible, invite someone from your local police or sheriff's department to come to your classroom and teach students to lift latent prints. They may be willing to share some of their real supplies with your students.

CSI in the Classroom

CSI Fingerprint Lab Sheet, Part II

rub
pencil
here

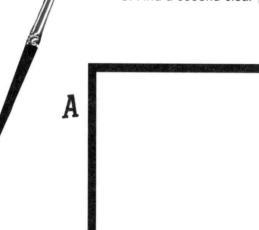

Directions:

1. Rub a number 2 pencil in the box at the top of this sheet until there is a dark smudge of graphite.

2. Your teacher has given you a glass. Wear gloves to handle it carefully, touching only the edges of the glass.

3. Use a magnifying glass to find one or more prints on the glass.

4. Rub the brush across the graphite until it is coated.

5. Gently brush the graphite across the fingerprint.

6. Carefully lay a piece of tape over the blackened fingerprint and lift it from the glass.

7. Place the tape with the print in box A below.

8. Find a second clear print, lift it, and place the tape in box B.

A  B

9. Examine the prints carefully. Compare them to the fingerprint templates of the other people in your group.

10. Try to identify the owner of the prints.

Name_____Date_____

CSI in the Classroom

CSI Bite Impressions Lab

Goal of this lab:

To take bite impressions and compare them to teeth marks left on objects or food items

Explanation:

Sometimes teeth marks are left on items at a crime scene. In this case, investigators would retrieve bite impressions from suspects and compare those to the evidence. This lab will give students experience in taking, examining, and comparing bite impressions. They will also use bite impressions to attempt to determine who bit a particular food item.

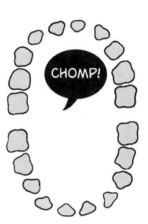

Materials needed:

- Styrofoam cups (one for each student)
- pens or pencils
- apples, small cubes of cheese, or another piece of Styrofoam
- glue or tape for mounting the Styrofoam onto the lab sheet template
- copies of Bite Impressions Lab Sheet

Directions:

1. Distribute a copy of the Bite Impression Lab Sheet and a Styrofoam cup to each student.

2. Review with the group the process for obtaining bite impressions, as described in instructions 1, 2, and 3 on the lab sheet.

3. Provide time for students to take impressions and mount them onto the lab sheet (instruction #4).

4. Direct them to complete instruction #5 on the lab sheet.

5. Put students into small groups. Pass apples, cheese cubes, and extra Styrofoam to each group. Have each person bite into a cube of cheese, an apple, or a piece of Styrofoam. They should then mix up the samples.

6. Direct groups to identify the teeth marks on each item.

7. Discuss this question with the entire group: How could teeth impressions help a CSI agent solve a crime?

8. Remind students that they would need an approved search warrant to obtain bite impressions from a suspect, just as they would need a warrant for fingerprints or any other item that could be evidence in a crime.

109

CSI Bite Impressions Lab Sheet

Directions:

1. Write your initials on the bottom of the cup.

2. Hold your cup to your mouth and carefully press the lip of the cup firmly into your bottom teeth. Carefully roll the cup to the left and then to the right. Beneath the bite impression, write the label, "Bottom Teeth."

3. On the opposite lip of the cup, repeat the process with your top teeth. Label that side, "Top Teeth."

4. Glue or tape the bitten sections of the cup to the template below.

5. Answer the following questions:

   A. How many teeth are present on the top impression? _____

   B. How many teeth are present on the bottom impression? _____

   C. How many crooked teeth marks do you see?_____Where?_____

   D. Compare your impressions with a partner. What are the similarities and differences? _____

_____

Bite Impressions Template	
Top Teeth	**Bottom Teeth**

Name_____Date_____

CSI in the Classroom

CSI Handwriting Lab

Meet me at Suzy's house at 1040 N. Wipple Ave.

Goals of this lab:

- to examine and analyze handwriting samples
- to compare handwriting samples for the purpose of identifying the writer of a particular sample

Explanation:

This lab gives students the opportunity to notice variations in handwriting styles and identify specific details of a person's handwriting. In addition, students can try to match handwriting from a mystery clue to the handwriting of known persons.

Materials needed:

- several half-sheets of paper
- magnifying glasses
- copies of CSI Handwriting Lab Sheets (parts I and II)
- pencils or pens
- handwriting samples

Lab Part I, Directions:

1. Give each student a copy of the lab sheet for Handwriting Lab Part I.
2. Give them time to complete 1 through 6. Discuss their observations.
3. Divide students into groups, giving paper and magnifying glasses to each.
4. Read the following instructions to students:
   Write your initials on the back of the paper. On the front, print or write in cursive the following: *"Meet me at Suzy's house at 1040 N. Wipple Ave."* Trade sheets within your group several times. Using your previous handwriting samples, try to determine whose new sheet you have.
5. Discuss the experience.

Lab Part II, Directions:

1. Give each student a copy of the lab sheet for Handwriting Lab Part II.
2. Review the directions with students.
3. Give them time to complete the task.
4. As a whole group, discuss students' observations and conclusions.
5. Encourage students to investigate graphology on the Internet.

CSI Handwriting Lab Sheet, Part I

Directions:

1. In the space below, print the following sentences neatly.

My name is George Smith. What is yours?

2. Now write those same sentences in your best cursive writing.

3. Identify some distinguishing or unique characteristics of your writing.

4. Identify some similarities and differences between the two samples.

5. Compare your samples with your neighbor's. Discuss the similarities and differences. Note distinguishing characteristics of each person's writing.

6. Get into your group and follow the teacher's instructions.

7. How could handwriting samples help a CSI agent solve a crime?

Name_____Date_____

CSI Handwriting Lab Sheet, Part II

A. Did Bill's monkey eat Lucy's gooey pizza?

B. Did Bill's monkey eat Lucy's gooey pizza?

C. Did Bill's monkey eat Lucy's gooey Pizza?

D. Did Bill's monkey eat lucy's gooey Pizza?

E. Did Bill's monkey eat Lucy's gooey pizza?

F. Did Bill's monkey eat Lucy's gooey pizza?

Directions:

1. The top of the page shows handwriting samples taken from six suspects. Pay attention to distinguishing characteristics of each sample.

2. Read the note below (found at a crime scene).

3. Use your observational skills to examine the note and the handwriting samples. Try to identify who wrote the note. (Your answer can be suspect A, B, C, D, E, F, or none of these.)

4. In your judgment, who wrote the note found at the crime scene?

5. What led you to this conclusion?

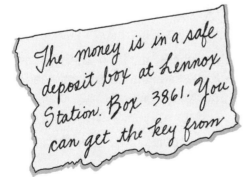

The money is in a safe deposit box at Lennox Station. Box 3861. You can get the key from

Name_____Date_____

CSI in the Classroom

CSI Mystery Substances Lab

Goal of this lab:

To learn to analyze some powders by mixing them with various liquids

Explanation:

A powder or other substance may be found at a crime scene. This becomes evidence that is tested in a lab to determine if it has any connection to the crime. Scientists and detectives compare test results of KNOWN substances to help identify UNKNOWN substances. In this lab, students gain experience in finding out how some known substances react with different liquids.

Materials needed:

- 8–10 cafeteria trays
- glue stick
- clear contact paper
- plastic wrap
- Popsicle sticks
- magnifying glasses

- eye droppers
- paper plates
- water
- vinegar
- iodine solution
- microscopes (optional)

- measuring spoons
- baking soda
- sugar
- baking powder
- cornstarch

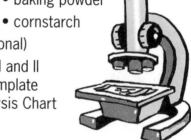

- Copies of: Mystery Substances Lab Sheets I and II
    Mystery Substances Lab Tray Template
    Mystery Substance Powder Analysis Chart

Directions:

1. Prepare 8 to 10 Mystery Substance Lab Trays using old cafeteria trays or laminated cardboard "trays." Follow the instructions on page 115.

2. Have all four powders and all three liquids available for students so they can access them easily. Provide eyedroppers for each liquid. **Caution: follow proper procedures when working with iodine.**

3. Provide four Popsicle sticks (stirring rods) for each group of students.

4. Before each use of a tray, cover it with plastic wrap. Then when it is time for cleanup, students place the Popsicle sticks in the center, pull the four corners of the plastic wrap together, and place it in a garbage can. Explain this procedure to students.

5. Arrange students into small groups. Supply copies of Lab Sheet I and the Powder Analysis Chart.

6. For a further Mystery Substance Lab experience, divide students into small groups again. Give each group copies of Lab Sheet II and a paper plate holding one of the four substances.

CSI Mystery Substances Lab Tray

Directions:

1. Make at least ten copies of this page.

2. Cut out the "cornstarch" strip and lightly glue it across the top of the tray.

3. Leave two inches below the "cornstarch" strip and glue the "baking powder" strip across the tray. Leave two inches and glue the "sugar" strip. Leave two inches and glue the "baking soda" strip.

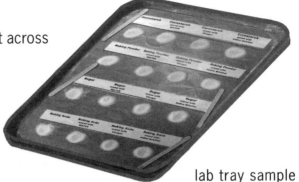

lab tray sample

4. Cover each tray with clear contact paper. This will protect the trays for future uses.

5. Before each lab use, cover trays with plastic wrap to provide for easy cleanup when the lab is finished.

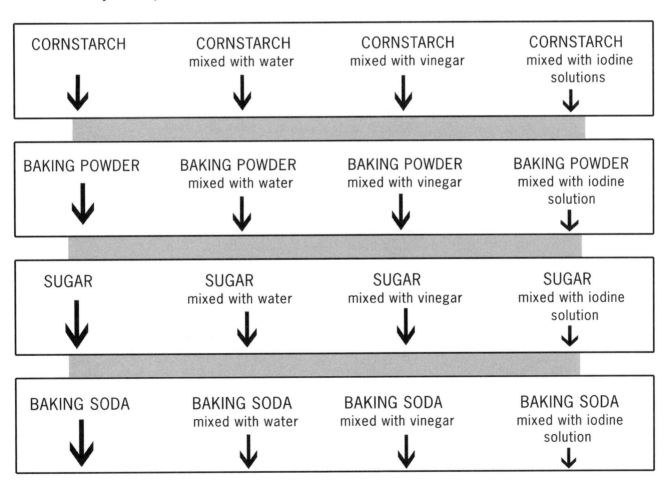

| CORNSTARCH ↓ | CORNSTARCH mixed with water ↓ | CORNSTARCH mixed with vinegar ↓ | CORNSTARCH mixed with iodine solutions ↓ |

| BAKING POWDER ↓ | BAKING POWDER mixed with water ↓ | BAKING POWDER mixed with vinegar ↓ | BAKING POWDER mixed with iodine solution ↓ |

| SUGAR ↓ | SUGAR mixed with water ↓ | SUGAR mixed with vinegar ↓ | SUGAR mixed with iodine solution ↓ |

| BAKING SODA ↓ | BAKING SODA mixed with water ↓ | BAKING SODA mixed with vinegar ↓ | BAKING SODA mixed with iodine solution ↓ |

CSI in the Classroom

CSI Mystery Substances
Lab Sheet I

Directions:

1. Place a teaspoon of the four white powders on a tray under the correct description. Caution: Do not taste any of the mystery substances. Never assume a substance is safe to taste—not even a tiny amount.

2. Study each powder with the magnifying glass. How would you describe the powder's shape? Does it have large or small grains? Write your observations in the "Appearance" column of the Powder Analysis Chart for each powder.

3. Rub each powder between your fingers. In the "Texture" column for each substance, describe how that powder feels.

4. Determine if there is a smell to any of the powders. Record your findings in the "Smell" column of the chart for each substance.

For the next three steps, use a separate stirring rod for each substance. Do not mix stirring rods with different substances.

5. Use the eyedropper to place 20 drops of water on each powder that says, "mixed with water." Do the powders dissolve? Is there a reaction? Write your observations in the "Reaction to Water" column for each substance.

6. Using the eyedropper, add 20 drops of vinegar to each substance that says, "mixed with vinegar." What happens? Record your observations in the "Reaction to Vinegar" column.

7. Caution: Iodine should be handled with care. Using the eyedropper, add 20 drops of iodine to each substance that says, "mixed with iodine solution." Record your observations in the "Reaction to Iodine Solution" column.

8. Go back and examine the chart. How many of the mixtures resulted in solutions? How many resulted in reactions?

Note: Comparing test results of known substances helps forensic scientists identify unknown substances.

Name _____ Date_____

CSI Powder Analysis Chart

Directions: Follow the procedures on Lab Sheet I. Record your observations on the chart.

Substances	Appearances	Texture	Smell	Reaction to Water	Reaction to Vinegar	Reaction to Iodine Solution
Cornstarch						
Baking Powder						
Sugar						
Baking Soda						

What physical properties do all four substances share?

_____

_____

_____

Name_____ Date_____

117

CSI in the Classroom

CSI Mystery Substances Lab Sheet II

Directions:

A white powder was found on the teacher's desk. A small portion of the powder was obtained on this paper plate for your group to test. Can you determine what this white substance is? Use the different solutions from the Mystery Substance Lab: water, vinegar, and iodine solution to help you solve this mystery. Use your Powder Analysis Chart also.

Caution: Do not put any substance in your mouth.

What is that white powder?

Answer: Based on our investigation, the mystery substance is

_____ .

Explain the procedures and observations used to arrive at

your answer._____

_____

_____

_____

_____

_____

_____

Group Members _____

_____

_____

Class_____   Date _____

CSI Chromatography Lab

Goals of this lab:
- to learn a simple chromatography method
- to use chromatography to compare ink samples

Explanation:
This lab explores a method that scientists use to separate components of a colored mixture such as ink, pigments, and dyes. Investigators and forensic scientists often use chromatography when trying to solve a crime.

Materials needed:
- 6 pens labeled A, B, C, D, E, F
- about 50 one-by-six-inch strips of coffee filter paper
- scissors, glue, and tape
- pencils
- 250 mL beakers
- copies of Chromatography Lab Sheet
- a mystery note written on coffee filter paper

Directions:

1. Before the lab, gather six different pens of the same color (such as felt tip pen, gel pen, ballpoint pen, fine tip permanent marker, etc.) Label them A–F with paper taped around the pen.

2. Test each pen before the lab. Choose one or more pens that stand out over the others and write several mystery notes with these pens on filter paper.

3. Set up a few different stations where the ink pens can be accessible for all students. At each station, have an example of a piece of filter paper labeled, with a pen line drawn on it. Tape these samples to the table or desk. Next to this, provide a supply of filter paper strips and a labeled pen.

4. Read the mystery note to the students. Tell them that they will use chromatography to figure out which pen wrote the note.

5. Divide students into small groups. Once in groups, students can begin following the directions on the lab sheets. After they have begun their work, give each student a mystery note to analyze.

Suspect Label	Draw a line with a sample pen.
	←

119

CSI Chromatography Lab Sheet

Directions:

1. Fill each of your 250 mL beakers with 25 mL of water.

2. Send someone to the station where Pen A is located. Label a strip of chromatography paper: "Suspect A." Draw a solid line with pen A about an inch from the bottom of the strip.

3. Repeat the procedure with the other five pens.

4. Fold the top edge of a strip over the pencil and tape it. Tape two strips to the same pencil.

5. Lay the pencil across a beaker, allowing the bottom edge of the strip to extend into the water. NOTE: It is VERY important that the pen line be ABOVE the water level. If this is not the case, get a new strip and draw the line up higher.

6. Let the strips stay in the water until the solvent (water) is about 6 cm from the original line. This could take about 10 to 15 minutes.

7. Describe your results for each pen on the chart. Glue a sample of each dried strip onto the appropriate box.

8. When the teacher gives you a mystery note, analyze the ink in the same way. Glue a dried sample into the box indicated.

9. Draw a conclusion as to which suspect wrote the note.

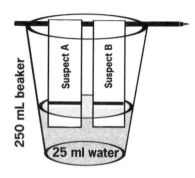

Glue a sample of the mystery note here.

SOLVENT	Suspect A	Suspect B	Suspect C	Suspect D	Suspect E	Suspect F
WATER						
Dry the paper strips. Glue a small sample in the box.						

Name_____Date_____

CSI Textiles Lab

Goals of this lab:

- to examine different textiles and identify characteristics
- to compare and contrast characteristics of textiles

Explanation:

The fiber characteristics of fabric or other textiles can be used as evidence to determine if a suspect or article was involved in a crime. Sometimes a clothing fiber or other textile substance is a major clue that helps to solve a crime. This lab allows students to observe and describe the properties and characteristics of different types of textiles. It also gives them experience using microscopes.

Materials needed:

- microscopes
- slides and cover plates
- scraps of four different textiles: nylon, cotton, silk, wool
- copies of Textiles Lab Sheet

Directions:

1. Review procedures for using microscopes and making slides. Practice the process of placing a substance on a microscope slide and securing it with a cover plate.

2. Cut small samples of each of the textiles, or pull fibers from each one.

3. Let students work to prepare slides of each textile. Prepare one set (of the four different textiles) for each microscope available. Make sure the slides are labeled.

4. Pass out copies of the Textiles Lab Sheet to students. Review the directions with them.

5. Explain a system (time and procedures) for each student to use a microscope to complete the lab activities.

6. Discuss the observations and comparisons.

CSI in the Classroom

CSI Textiles Lab Sheet

Directions:

1. Carefully examine each textile sample. Notice properties and characteristics.

2. Draw the sample in the appropriate circle. Be sure to note the magnification.

3. Beneath each drawing, write a brief description of properties that you observe.

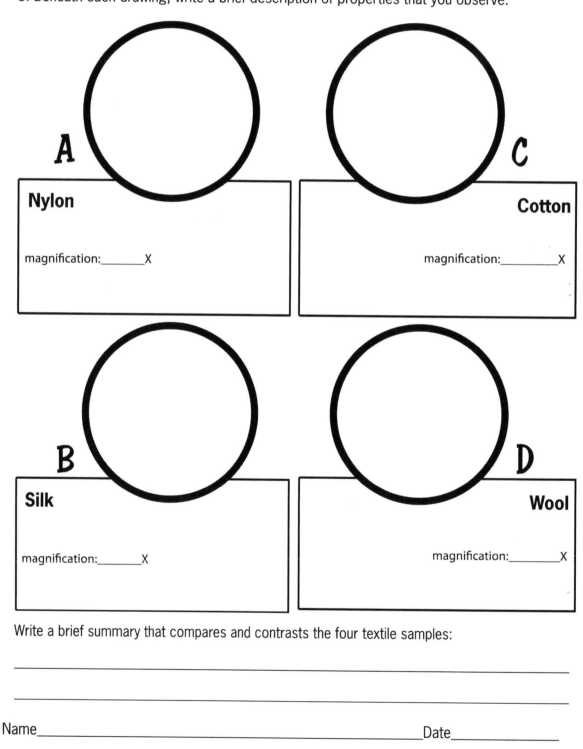

A

Nylon

magnification:_____X

C

Cotton

magnification:_____X

B

Silk

magnification:_____X

D

Wool

magnification:_____X

Write a brief summary that compares and contrasts the four textile samples:

_____

_____

Name_____ Date_____

CSI Resources

CRIME SCENE DO NOT CROSS CRIME SCENE DO NOT

Frequently Asked Questions
About CSI

Excellent Websites for CSI

CSI T-Shirt

Frequently Asked Questions About

1. How can I adapt the CSI idea to my subject area?

A classroom CSI may seem like a science unit. Certainly, there are many ways that science processes and skills can be taught, strengthened, and made relevant through a CSI unit. If you don't teach science, take these steps to adapt the unit to your discipline.

A. Think about CSI this way: the scientific inquiry process is critical thinking at its best! Look closely at the skills involved in a CSI unit (page 8) and identify those that your students need to work on anyway.

B. When you create the scenario, concoct a crime that needs your content area skills in order to reach a solution. For example,

Math – Include clues or crimes that use measurement, operations with money, calculations, time, temperature, algebra, or geometry.

Language Arts – Emphasize the reading, writing, listening, and speaking skills that are already involved. Enhance the language arts aspect by adding clues that require critical reading or examination and analysis of media information.

Social Studies – Include historical or geographical concepts in the scenario. Design clues that require students to find or review historical events and facts, explain core democratic values, locate places or spaces on maps, investigate climatic issues such as tide changes and currents, or understand workings of the government.

P.E. – Include places, events, or sports that require physical activities to solve the crime. Use clues that only make sense when investigators understand principles of exercise, body function, nutrition, or other P.E. concepts.

Art – Include principles of art analysis or facts of art history in the crime. Require the use of art supplies and processes to report, describe, or explain the results of the investigation.

Music or Drama – Include clues that can only be sorted out with knowledge of musical concepts or theatrical terminology. Make these performing arts a part of the reporting process. Students can describe their investigation and results by creating musical or movement representations.

2. Are there other things besides prelabs that get students ready for CSI?

Certainly, you can prime the excitement with resources related to mysteries, detective work, and crime-scene investigation. This includes stories, video clips, real-life news reports, field trips, and visits to the classroom from people whose professions are relevant. You can also sharpen skills that will be needed for the CSI. Brainstorm interview questions and practice interviewing techniques. Review processes of reporting and summarizing. Practice analysis of written reports, news reports, or oral accounts of events. Discuss bias and identify ways it can get in the way of objective analysis. Look at that list of skills on page 8 of this book. Practicing any of these ahead of time will benefit your investigators.

3. Are there guidelines for choosing suspects?

Think about the possible suspects before you settle on a scenario. Choose people who could logically be connected to the crime or to the location of one crime scene. Also, it is a good idea to choose suspects whose jobs and schedules allow them to be available for interviews, fingerprinting, and other CSI contacts.

4. What happens if students identify dozens of suspects?

Give the students a couple of days to consider who the suspects might be. As they interview the victim, they will stumble across names of possible witnesses who may identify other suspects. Many of the suspects on their lists will "fall off" once they are interviewed, because it will become clear that they have alibis. Obviously, you cannot let the suspect list get out of hand. Emphasize the idea that there must be some strong cause to suspect someone. After students have had time to discuss possibilities and conduct some interviews, share your list of suspects with them. Try to steer them toward the suspects you have chosen.

5. There's a lot going on in the CSI! Won't things get chaotic?

Yes, a CSI unit is a busy event. Students are so motivated and so involved that things are more "busily productive" than "chaotic." To avoid chaos:

- Make procedures clear and easy to follow.
- Review all forms thoroughly with students before they go to work on them.
- Set clear expectations for behavior during the CSI. Hold students to the expectations—starting with the prelabs.
- Start every CSI day with a meeting. Use this time to review expectations, answer questions, solve any problems, and clarify the tasks for the day.
- Keep strong limits on the number of students out of the classroom at once.
- Examine CSI team folders at the end of the day to keep tabs on how teams are doing and catch any problems before they become severe.

6. Is there an arrest?

There can be, if you choose to include this. The teacher can announce the guilty suspect after the final reports are reviewed. The "arrest" can be fictional, or you can arrange for something to happen. When final reports are finished, you will probably find differences in conclusions as to who is guilty. Some teams may write excellent reports, but follow the evidence to the wrong person. Others may have the right suspect, but provide minimal evidence. Discuss these situations fully so that teams understand how the evidence was insufficient or how the conclusions were wrongly drawn.

7. What do students in the classroom do while others are out investigating?

Don't worry that there will be nothing to do. There is plenty for them to do. This is different, of course, at different points in the investigation. Remaining team members can draft questions for suspects; write up results of interviews; describe reasons for suspecting someone; summarize alibis; write search warrant affidavits; work on defining terms; explore Internet sites; analyze, describe, and discuss evidence; work on reports or parts of reports; perfect the scale drawings or models; perform labs; and test out different theories about the crime.

8. Isn't it hard for students to get accurate fingerprints?

Lifting fingerprints is fascinating and fun, but can be messy and give inaccurate results. Keep a close watch on this, and give assistance when necessary. Some teachers use the fingerprint evidence tags obtained from the suspects before the CSI, "trading" them with tags in team folders so that students have the correct prints. Let students have the experience, but do all you can to make it successful. Make sure suspect fingerprints at the crime scenes are very clear. Redo these at the end of the day, if necessary, so the teams have clean prints the next day.

9. How long should a CSI unit last?

This will vary, depending on how long it takes for the students to do the investigation. The average is about three weeks. Watch the progress of the teams. Do not let the CSI drag on too long, but give enough time for them to carefully collect and analyze evidence, write reports, and draw conclusions.

10. Should I give grades for the CSI unit? If so, how?

There is no one right answer to this question. It depends on your goals for the unit and your class evaluation system. In making this decision, think about the purpose of the grade and the way you evaluate performance for other units. What do you hope to accomplish by giving a grade?

A CSI unit, however small, is a big deal in most classrooms. Ordinarily, students dedicate serious work and commitment to a CSI unit. So it should be considered the "real thing" in terms of learning. Students deserve some kind of evaluative feedback, whether it be by self-evaluation, peer evaluation, teacher evaluation, or some combination of these. If there is no feedback that comes as some kind of assessment, students may view the CSI as just a fun "extra" rather than as an integral part of their class learning. In addition, the student needs some sort of measure of how well goals of the CSI were accomplished.

There are many forms of assessment that will work. The CSI Scoring Rubric can serve as a guideline for your evaluation. The total score can be converted to a letter grade, if you wish. The chart here shows how one teacher made the conversion. Some teachers use the team score as a portion of a grade, and then add other components of evaluation for individual students.

Sample conversion to grades: 200 points
200 – 185 = A
184 – 179 = A–
178 – 174 = B+
173 – 165 = B
164 – 159 = B–
158 – 155 = C+
154 – 145 = C
144 – 139 = C–
134 – 125 = D
138 – 135 = D+
124 – 119 = D–
118 – below + NC

Excellent Websites for CSI

Here are some websites that I have used successfully with my students. They offer some wonderful support to a classroom CSI unit.

Use preparation and caution with any Internet search. Review all websites thoroughly and regularly before sending students to visit them. Use sites from reputable organizations only. And check the sites regularly. Sites change material frequently, so the unit or article listed may be gone at a later date. And web addresses are often closed down or sold to other users. A site that is appropriate today might be something entirely different in a few months.

Whodunnit
http://www.geocities.com/sseagraves/whodunnit.htm
- The lessons are divided into three areas:
  Mysteries in Literature   Critical Thinking Skills   Forensic Science

TRU TV (formerly Court TV): Forensics in the Classroom
http://www.trutv.com/forensics_curriculum/
- "The Backpack Mystery" is a great 50-minute read as a pre-CSI activity; students read through it and try to figure out at the end who did it.

How Stuff Works: Forensics Science
http://science.howstuffworks.com/forensic-science-channel.htm

FBI Kids Page
http://www.fbi.gov/kids/k5th/kidsk5th.htm
http://www.fbi.gov/fbikids.htm

Science News for kids
http://www.sciencenewsforkids.org/articles/20041215/TZWorksheet.asp
- Worksheet for the crime lab article

http://www.sciencenewsforkids.org/articles/20041215/Feature1.asp
- Article about crime labs

The Science Spot: Forensic Science Lesson Plans
http://www.sciencespot.net/Pages/classforsci.html#crimescene
- Daily CSI Challenges
- Lessons and units on such topics as Crime Scene Basics, Eyewitnesses, Power of Evidence, Blood Basics, Fingerprint Basics, Arson Investigation, and Accident Reconstruction
- List of supply companies for forensic supplies

The CSI T-Shirt

Make T-shirts as a kick-off or culminating activity for your CSI.

Students can:

- design their own and make T-shirts in the classroom

- design their own and take the design to a T-shirt shop for transfer

- use the design on this page to transfer and iron onto T-shirts

- take the design on this page to a T-shirt shop for transfer

CSI

in the Classroom